Problematic Research Practices and Inertia in Scientific Psychology

This volume explores the abiding intellectual inertia in scientific psychology in relation to the discipline's engagement with problematic beliefs and assumptions underlying mainstream research practices, despite repeated critical analyses which reveal the weaknesses, and in some cases complete inappropriateness, of these methods. Such paradigmatic inertia is especially troublesome for a scholarly discipline claiming status as a science.

The book offers penetrating analyses of many (albeit not all) of the most important areas where mainstream practices require either compelling justifications for their continuation or adjustments – possibly including abandonment – toward more apposite alternatives. Specific areas of concern addressed in this book include the systemic misinterpretation of statistical knowledge; the prevalence of a conception of measurement at odds with yet purporting to mimic the natural sciences; the continuing widespread reliance on null hypothesis testing; and the continuing resistance within psychology to the explicit incorporation of qualitative methods into its methodological toolbox. Broader level chapters examine mainstream psychology's systemic disregard for critical analysis of its tenets, and the epistemic and ethical problems this has created.

This is a vital and engaging resource for researchers across psychology, and those in the wider behavioural and social sciences who have an interest in, or who use, psychological research methods.

James T. Lamiell retired in 2017 after 42 years as a university professor. 36 of those years were spent at Georgetown University, USA. His scholarly work has long been concentrated in the history and philosophy of psychology, with interests in psychological research methodology and in the works of the German philosopher and psychologist William Stern (1871–1938).

Kathleen L. Slaney is a professor in the Department of Psychology at Simon Fraser University, Canada. She is a Fellow of the American Psychological Association. Her research has focused primarily on psychological meta-science.

Advances in Theoretical and Philosophical Psychology
Series Editor
Brent D. Slife
Brigham Young University

Editorial Board

Advances in Theoretical and Philosophical Psychology
Series Editor
Brent D. Slife
Brigham Young University

Nancy K. Dess
A Multidisciplinary Approach to Embodiment: Understanding Human Being

Jack Martin
From Scientific Psychology to the Study of Persons: A Psychologist's Memoir

James T. Lamiell and Kathleen L. Slaney
Problematic Research Practices and Inertia in Scientific Psychology: History, Sources, and Recommended Solutions

www.routledge.com/psychology/series/TPP

Problematic Research Practices and Inertia in Scientific Psychology

History, Sources, and
Recommended Solutions

**Edited by James T. Lamiell
and Kathleen L. Slaney**

Routledge
Taylor & Francis Group

LONDON AND NEW YORK

First published 2021
by Routledge
2 Park Square, Milton Park, Abingdon, Oxon OX14 4RN

and by Routledge
52 Vanderbilt Avenue, New York, NY 10017

Routledge is an imprint of the Taylor & Francis Group, an informa business

British Library Cataloguing-in-Publication Data
A catalogue record for this book is available from the British Library

Library of Congress Cataloging-in-Publication Data
Names: Lamiell, James T., editor. | Slaney, Kathleen L. editor.
Title: Scientific psychology's problematic research practices
and inertia : history, sources, and recommended solutions /
edited by James T. Lamiell and Kathleen L. Slaney.
Description: Abingdon, Oxon ; New York, NY : Routledge, 2021. |
Series: Advances in theoretical and philosophical psychology |
Includes bibliographical references and index.
Identifiers: LCCN 2020029585 (print) | LCCN 2020029586 (ebook) |
ISBN 9780367644864 (hardback) | ISBN 9780367644871 (paperback) |
ISBN 9781003124757 (ebook)
Subjects: LCSH: Psychology–Research–Moral and
ethical aspects. | Psychology–Research–Methodology.
Classification: LCC BF76.4 .S345 2021 (print) |
LCC BF76.4 (ebook) | DDC 150.72–dc23
LC record available at https://lccn.loc.gov/2020029585
LC ebook record available at https://lccn.loc.gov/2020029586

ISBN: 978-0-367-64486-4 (hbk)
ISBN: 978-1-003-12475-7 (ebk)

Typeset in Times New Roman
by Newgen Publishing UK

To the memory of Rom Harré (1927–2019), prolific scholar, patient mentor, enthusiastic teacher, and dear colleague.

Contents

viii   *Contents*

Contributors

James W. Grice is Professor of psychology at Oklahoma State University where he has taught courses in statistics, personality, psychological testing, and personalism for the past fourteen years. He is author of Idiogrid, a program for personality assessment currently in use in over 30 countries around the world. He is also author of *Observation Oriented Modeling: Analysis of Cause in the Behavioral Sciences* (2011) and the accompanying OOM software.

Fiona J. Hibberd is Senior Lecturer in the School of Psychology at the University of Sydney. She specializes in the assumptions that underpin research in psychology and is the author of journal articles about the relationships between psychology and various philosophies of science and the book *Unfolding Social Constructionism* (2005).

Richard E. Hohn is a doctoral student in the psychology department, Simon Fraser University. His research interests include the philosophical issues related to psychological measurement and test validity theory, as well as applied psychometrics, data analysis, and data visualization.

Rafaële Huntjens is an associate professor at the department of clinical psychology and experimental psychopathology, University of Groningen, the Netherlands. The main focus in her work is on cognitive-behavioral processes in trauma-related disorders with a specific emphasis on dissociative disorders.

Hailey Johnson recently graduated from Oklahoma State University with a BS in Psychology. Hailey will shortly be embarking on a Master of Social Work degree at the University of Oklahoma. Her research interests include coping skills for children who have faced trauma early on in their development.

James T. Lamiell retired in 2017 after 42 years as a university professor, 36 at Georgetown University. His scholarly work has long been concentrated in the history and philosophy of psychology, with particular interests in psychological research methodology and in the works of the German philosopher and psychologist William Stern (1871–1938). He is a Fellow of the American Psychological Association and former President of APA Divisions 24 and 26.

Jack Martin is Professor Emeritus of Psychology at Simon Fraser University. He is a Fellow of the Canadian and American Psychological Associations, former President of the Society for Theoretical and Philosophical Psychology (STPP), and recipient of the STPP's Award for Distinguished Lifetime Contributions to Theoretical and Philosophical Psychology.

Lisa M. Osbeck is a professor of Psychology at the University of West Georgia. She is interested in both the philosophy and psychology of science, especially concerning the personhood of scientists and interdisciplinary collaboration. Authored books are *Values in Psychological Science: Re-imagining Epistemic Priorities at a New Frontier* (2019) and *Science as Psychology: Sense-Making and Identity in Science Practice* (with N. Nersessian, K. Malone, & W. Newstetter; 2011). Edited volumes are *Rational Intuition: Philosophical Roots, Scientific Investigations*, with Barbara Held (2014) and *Psychological Studies of Science and Technology*, with Kieran O'Doherty, Ernst Schraube, and Jeffrey Yen (2019).

Kathleen L. Slaney is a professor in the department of psychology at Simon Fraser University. Her research has focused primarily on psychological meta-science and conceptual analysis of psychological concepts. She is a Fellow of the American Psychological Association. She is author of *Validating Psychological Constructs* and co-editor of *A Wittgensteinian Perspective on the Use of Conceptual Analysis in Psychology* and *The Wiley Handbook of Theoretical Psychology*.

Donna Tafreshi is an assistant professor of psychology at the University of the Fraser Valley in British Columbia, Canada, where she teaches courses on methods, history, and philosophy of psychology. Her scholarly work focuses on analyzing the historical and conceptual foundations of methodological approaches and their social and scientific consequences.

Series Foreword

Brent D. Slife, Editor

Psychologists need to face the facts. Their commitment to empiricism for answering disciplinary questions does not prevent pivotal questions from arising that cannot be evaluated exclusively through empirical methods, hence the title of this series: *Advances in Theoretical and Philosophical Psychology*. For example, such moral questions as, "What is the nature of a good life?" are crucial to psychotherapists but are not answerable through empirical methods alone. And what of the methods themselves? Many have worried that our current psychological means of investigation are not adequate for fully understanding the person (e.g., Schiff, 2019). How do we address this concern through empirical methods without running headlong into the dilemma of methods investigating themselves? Such questions are in some sense philosophical, to be sure, but the discipline of psychology cannot advance even its own empirical agenda without addressing questions like these in defensible ways.

How then should the discipline of psychology deal with such distinctly theoretical questions? We could leave the answers exclusively to professional philosophers, but this option would mean that the conceptual foundations of the discipline, including the conceptual framework of empiricism itself, are left to scholars who are *outside* the discipline. As undoubtedly helpful as philosophers are and will be, this situation would mean that the people doing the actual psychological work, psychologists themselves, are divorced from the people who formulate and re-formulate the conceptual foundations of that work. This division of labor would not seem to serve the long-term viability of the discipline.

Instead, the founders of psychology – thinkers such as Wundt, Freud, and James – recognized the importance of psychologists in formulating their own foundations. These parents of psychology not only did their own theorizing, in cooperation with many other disciplines; they also realized the significance of psychologists continuously *re*-examining these theories and philosophies. This re-examination process allowed for the people most directly involved in and knowledgeable about the discipline to be the ones to decide *whether* changes were needed and *how* such changes would best be implemented. This book series is dedicated to that task, the examining and re-examining of psychology's foundations.

Reference

Schiff, B. (2019). *Situating qualitative methods in psychological science.* London: Routledge.

1   Introduction

James T. Lamiell and Kathleen L. Slaney

As the title of this volume indicates, our core concern here is with an abiding intellectual inertia in the discipline of scientific psychology. This inertia is reflected in the continued prevalence of beliefs and assumptions that have guided research methods and justified psychologists' practical interventions for decades, despite repeated critical analyses revealing the weaknesses—and, in some instances, complete inappropriateness—of those beliefs and assumptions. Occasionally, but far too infrequently, advocates of the critiqued assumptions have attempted to refute the critics, but, routinely, the insufficiencies of the putative refutations have in turn been pointed out by the critics, leaving the critiques fully in force. Nevertheless, the problematic beliefs and assumptions have continued to dominate within the mainstream of the field, much as if no critiques had never even been mounted. In short, apart from the infrequent and consistently unsuccessful attempts at refutation just mentioned, the response within the mainstream to the critiques has been to simply *ignore* them. Paradigmatic inertia of the sort reflected by these developments would be intellectually untoward for any scholarly discipline, but it is especially problematic for one claiming status as a science.

A discussion sharing concerns along this line took place in a session of the 2018 midwinter conference of the Society for Theoretical and Philosophical Psychology (Division 24 of the American Psychological Association), held in Phoenix, Arizona. Contributions to this volume have been made by all five participants in that session: James Grice, Richard Hohn, and Jack Martin, in addition to the two individuals who have coauthored this chapter and coedited the volume. This work also contains chapters by two individuals, Donna Tafreshi and Fiona Hibberd, who were not present for the session in Phoenix but had relevant contributions to make. Finally, Lisa Osbeck's concluding chapter offers a thoughtful critical perspective on each of the other seven contributions and on the volume as a whole.

In what follows, we provide a concise preview of each of the seven topical chapters, discussed in the order in which they have been organized in this book.

A condensed preview of the topical chapters

On the systemic misuse of statistical methods within mainstream psychology

Lamiell's chapter reiterates his long-running argument against interpreting knowledge of statistical relationships between variables defined only for aggregates of individuals as if it constituted knowledge of the individuals within the aggregates. The chapter provides an overview of key historical developments behind the institutionalization of the field's problematic interpretive practices, and then explains the inadequacy of recent attempts to defend those practices by invoking (a) probabilistic thinking and/or (b) considerations of practical utility. The thesis is reasserted that knowledge of statistical relationships among variables marking differences between individuals is properly regarded as knowledge of populations and not knowledge of *any* single one of the individuals within those populations. Such knowledge is, literally, knowledge of *no one,* and this is true whether the between-person differences being statistically examined are differences that have been captured by tests of one sort or another, as in correlational studies, or differences that have been created through investigator-imposed treatments, as in true experiments. Lamiell contends that through the long-prevalent indulgence of inappropriate interpretations of aggregate statistical knowledge, mainstream thinkers within scientific psychology have gradually but effectively, even if unwittingly, transformed the field into a species of demography he calls 'psycho-demography,' and he mourns the persistence within the field, over many decades, of a quite deliberate 'ignore-ance' of this conceptual reality and its full implications.

Psychology's inertia: Epistemological and ethical implications

Hibberd's contribution takes aim at the persistence of a positivistic ethos within psychology despite the recognition long ago in other disciplines of positivism's failure as a philosophy of science. The enduring positivistic ethos in psychology, Hibberd argues, sustains psychology's defective concepts of method and evidence, the false scientific claims that those concepts sanction, misguided research questions and interpretations of results, and, what is perhaps most problematic in the long run, an inadequate system of self-correction. Hibberd argues forcefully that attempts at redress have repeatedly fallen on deaf ears, while a seemingly ingrained not-wanting-to-know—more of the deliberate 'ignore-ance' mentioned above—prevails instead. This, Hibberd contends, is unethical and contrary to the disinterested truth-seeking which is a hallmark of genuinely scientific inquiry. Importantly, Hibberd suggests some actions that could help to remediate these serious conceptual problems within psychology and, in the process, enhance the discipline's integrity and scientific maturity.

Intransigence in mainstream thinking about psychological measurement

Hohn's focus is on the inertia that has existed for decades within mainstream psychology in the domain of measurement practices. In his chapter, he leads the reader through a discussion of a series of missteps that have occurred within the field, beginning in the late 19th century with the work of the psychophysicists and continuing through the 20th century and now into the 21st. As those missteps unfolded, psychology's accepted measurement practices became widely discrepant from those prevailing in the natural sciences that, ironically, psychology has all along seen itself as emulating. Although critical expositions of that untoward development have been offered in recent decades, the critiques have largely been ignored, and, today, the questionable assumptions and practices remain firmly entrenched within the field. In his treatment of these matters, Hohn pays particular attention to the relevant efforts of the contemporary Australian scholar Joel Michell.

Persistent disregard for the inadequacies of null hypothesis significance testing and the viable alternative of observation-oriented modeling

Despite a sizable extant literature discussing the problems with null hypothesis significance testing (NHST) as a methodological vehicle for advancing the agenda of psychological science, the practice continues to prevail within the field as the investigative paradigm of choice. In their chapter, Grice, Huntjens, and Johnson draw attention once again to that literature, and to Grice's own efforts, begun over a decade ago, to develop an alternative framework that would not only avoid the major problems with NHST, but would, in the process, enable investigators to actually accomplish much that most have mistakenly believed has been and is being accomplished with NHST. Despite Grice's efforts to establish the framework he calls Observation-Oriented Modeling (OOM), however, mainstream inquiry remains dominated by NHST. Persisting in his efforts to overcome this inertia, Grice and his coauthors discuss in this chapter how concepts in OOM can be used to expand upon or supplant contemporary understandings of effect size, causality, measurement, and inference. These authors then bring the conceptual and analytic tools of OOM to bear in a reanalysis of the findings of a previously published paper on inter-identity amnesia in persons diagnosed with Dissociative Identity Disorder.

On the interpretive nature of quantitative methods and psychology's resistance to qualitative methods

Tafreshi's contribution to this volume addresses the long-standing and continuing resistance within the mainstream of psychology to the use of qualitative methods. Historically, this resistance has been grounded in the belief that the adoption of qualitative methods would compromise psychology's status as a science. Tafreshi's core thesis is that the roots of that resistance are to be found in inadequate education and training in *quantitative* methods. She advances that thesis by showing the various ways in which the exercise of quantitative methods in psychology, both in the domain of measurement and in the domain of statistical analysis, necessarily incorporates considerations of a fundamentally qualitive nature. She argues that if quantitative methodological approaches were taught to psychology students in a way that emphasizes rather than obscures the interpretative role of the investigator, the inevitable presence of qualitative considerations in *all* psychological research, including research that incorporates quantitative methods, would be more apparent. This, in turn, would incline coming generations of psychological researchers to be more receptive to the larger possibilities offered by qualitative methods for expanding scientific psychology's methodological toolbox.

Is there a waning appetite for critical methodology in psychology?

Slaney begins her chapter by noting that, over the years, there has, in fact, been an appreciable amount of scrutiny by critically oriented psychologists of the assumptions and beliefs of their discipline's prevailing research methods and practices. Unfortunately, she argues, those discussions seem to have had little impact on those working 'in the trenches' of psychological research and practice. She is thus led to wonder about the nature and sources of this disconnect. After briefly surveying the history of major critical efforts in psychology, Slaney moves into a discussion of the ways in which psychological science does and does not appear to be methodologically inert. Her analysis is organized around two broad types of methodological critique: *restitutive* and *radical*. Critiques of the former type are aimed at achieving correctives in certain of mainstream psychology's methodological practices without challenging the very methodological foundation of the discipline. Radical methodological critiques, by contrast, strike at just those methodological foundations, often promoting fundamentally different approaches to psychological inquiry. Slaney offers for consideration various exemplars of each of these two types of critique, as well as her assessment of their relative (in)effectiveness to date in leading to disciplinary changes.

Psychology's struggle with understanding persons

In what would well qualify as a radical critique in Slaney's framework, Martin argues that the research methods that have long dominated mainstream psychology must finally be recognized as fundamentally ill-suited for a psychology that would aim toward an understanding of particular persons. Complementing Lamiell's argument (refer above) that psycho-demographic knowledge is, effectively, knowledge of *no one*, and working in the intellectual patrimony of such well-known predecessors such Wilhelm Dilthey (1833–1911), Wilhelm Windelband (1848–1915), William Stern (1871–1938), Gordon Allport (1897–1967), and others, Martin contends that the sampling and statistical methods of most psychological research impede rather than facilitate an understanding of individual persons, i.e., entities that are (or once were) living, breathing *some ones*. Such an understanding, to the extent that it can be achieved at all, requires biographical work that illuminates the makeup of real persons' lives as they are actually lived. Resistance within the mainstream to views of the sort expressed by Martin has prevailed within mainstream thinking at least since the time shortly before the turn of the 20th century when Hermann Ebbinghaus (1850–1909) directly rebutted Dilthey's call for a *verstehende* or 'understanding' psychology modeled on the human sciences (*Geisteswissenschaften*). Ebbinghaus firmly defended an *erklärende* or 'explanatory' psychology devoted to the search for general laws on the model of the natural sciences (*Naturwissenschaften*). In a very real sense, therefore, Martin's thesis represents a vision for scientific psychology that has been defended by a small minority of psychologists virtually from the outset of the time in the late 19th century when the field was formally established as an independent scientific discipline in the laboratories of Wilhelm Wundt

(1832–1920) at the University of Leipzig. For just as long a time, however, mainstream resistance to this vision has been firm, even though mainstream psychology continues to have precious little to show by way of accomplishments on the order to those that have been achieved in the natural sciences.

In her clear and cogent commentary, Lisa Osbeck identifies how the individual contributors to this volume address in common what putatively are the core problems of psychology, and gives reasons and potential solutions for these problems. However, Osbeck illuminates the differences across the individual chapters in terms of which problems are emphasized and which reasons and solutions are offered. Osbeck astutely recognizes the need for the contributors to not fall prey to diagnosing what is in large part a feature of a system that sustains erroneous or ill-fitting methods and practices as an illness suffered only or primarily by individual researchers. Osbeck also appeals for the accompaniment to critique of constructive alternatives, such as Grice's OOM, a concrete and salient application of which is featured in Chapter 5.

A call for critical responsiveness

We noted at the outset of our discussion that this work arose out of concern over the widespread and long-standing indifference within the mainstream of scientific psychology to penetrating critical analyses of certain of the disciplines most fundamental tenets and investigative practices. Our objective has been to gather into a single volume forceful statements of several different scholars documenting this indifference, and drawing attention to its untoward consequences both for the discipline of scientific psychology itself and, in turn, for the people whose lives are impacted by the knowledge claims invoked by applied psychologists to justify their interventions.

The contributors to this volume harbor no illusion that it will, by some mysterious force, immediately overcome the inertia that has dominated within the mainstream for a great many decades. We do hope, however, that the critical analyses offered here will finally receive the commensurately critical consideration that they have long deserved. Should such consideration reveal the faultiness or otherwise problematic nature of a critic's arguments, we hope that there will soon appear carefully crafted rejoinders explaining just why this has been seen to be the case.

By the same token, we hope that where careful critical consideration forces recognition of the validity of the critics' original arguments, acknowledgments of same will likewise soon be forthcoming, followed in due course by the implementation of the changes mandated by the critiques: in research methods, in interventions and other practical applications, and in the textbooks and other materials that will be used to train future generations of psychologists and to communicate the works of the discipline to interested others situated beyond the field's borders but standing to benefit from the field's scientific accomplishments.

Our broader hope for this volume is that it will help to revive within the discipline of psychology an appreciation of the inevitable need within this or any other scientific discipline for continuous critical reflection on its basic assumptions and methodological practices, and in the process expel the deliberate 'ignore-ance' that now so widely prevails. We firmly believe that if change of this nature can finally occur, psychology will be improved both as a basic scientific discipline and as field of professional practice.

2 On the systemic misuse of statistical methods within mainstream psychology

James T. Lamiell

The concern in this chapter is with the troubling inertia among mainstream psychological investigators in the face of repeated critiques of the long-standing practice of regarding statistical knowledge of populations as if it warrants claims to scientific knowledge about the psychological functioning of individuals within those populations. The problematic nature of this common interpretive (mal)practice has been pointed out in various ways in publications dating at least to the middle of the 20th century. Scholar David Bakan (1921–2004) discussed the problem in terms of a widespread conflation by researchers of knowledge of the *general* with knowledge of the *aggregate* (cf. Bakan, 1955, 1966). As he correctly stated, "the use of methods which are appropriate to [gaining] the [former] type [of knowledge] in the establishment and confirmation of the [latter] leads to error" (Bakan, 1955, p. 211, brackets added). Bakan's admonitions were widely ignored.

Subsequently, the well-known research methodologist, Fred N. Kerlinger (1910–1991), discussed in a 1979 text what he termed a "troublesome paradox" in much psychological research, created by treating group-level statistical findings as informative about the individual-level 'doings' of theoretical and/or practical interest (Kerlinger, 1979, p. 275). Although Kerlinger (1979) did not cite Bakan (1955, 1966), the conceptual problem Kerlinger identified is the direct consequence of the very conflation Bakan had discussed. Like Bakan, however, Kerlinger, too, was ignored—even, as it turns out, by himself, as he paid no further attention to the 'conceptual paradox' in the research methods text he published seven years later (Kerlinger, 1986).

Revisiting in 1981 what is essentially the same problem, the present author drew attention to mainstream 'personality' psychologists' fallacious practice of interpreting of correlational indices of the reliability and validity of personality tests as empirical grounds for empirically evaluating the theoretical assumption of temporal and trans-situational consistency in the manifestation by individuals of their respective traits (Lamiell, 1981). That publication was followed by numerous works, published periodically over the next four decades (cf. Lamiell, 1987, 1997, 2003, 2015, 2016), elaborating, from a variety of angles, on the problematic nature of established interpretive practices in both correlational and experimental studies (e.g., Lamiell, 2019). Yet, false interpretations of aggregate statistical knowledge have continued—indeed, have proliferated—while the critiques of those interpretations have been, for the most part, simply ignored (see, e.g., the commentary by Rom Harré (1927–2019) on the imperviousness of mainstream personality investigators to the various critiques just cited; Harré, 2006).

The conceptual problems here are fundamentally epistemic: fallacious interpretations of aggregate statistical findings result in unjustified claims to scientific knowledge about individuals. This is bad science.[1] Beyond that, however: when those ill-founded knowledge claims are exercised in the applied domain in order to justify interventions in the lives of individuals, the problems take on a socio-ethical dimension as well (cf. Lamiell, 2019, chapter 6). It is to be hoped, therefore, that the present discussion, though necessarily brief, will prompt readers who remain oblivious to these critical discussions or skeptical of their merits to finally consider or reconsider, thoughtfully and in duly critical fashion, a more detailed examination of the relevant issues that can be found elsewhere (Lamiell, 2019). In that work, the various facets of the problem are explored in greater detail and depth than is possible here.

The present chapter offers a highly condensed treatment of the nature and historical development of the problem. This is followed by a discussion of the inadequacy of certain attempted rebuttals of the critique that have been reiterated in recent publications (Banicki, 2018; Proctor and Xiong, 2018).

The influx and proliferation of aggregate statistical methods in psychology: A brief review of some key historical developments

The aggregate statistical methods that have come to thoroughly dominate research practices within the mainstream of scientific psychology played no role in the experimental psychology famously pioneered by Wilhelm Wundt (1832–1920) in Leipzig in 1879. That discipline was oriented toward the discovery of lawful regularities in various aspects of psychological functioning (e.g., sensations, perceptions, judgments, memories, and other psychological processes) that would be *general* in the sense of *common to all* of the individuals investigated. Precisely because "*each individual* [was to be regarded as] *a particular in which the general is manifest*" (Bakan, 1966, p. 433, emphasis in original, brackets added), experiments had to be conducted in such a way that the findings would be completely specifiable for each investigated individual. In other words, the original general-experimental psychology had to be prosecuted on what would be called, in modern parlance, an "N = 1" basis. This fact is reflected in the frequent references one can find in the literature of the day to the 'general-experimental-*individual*' psychology (see, e.g., Stern, 1900; Wundt, 1912; cf. Lamiell, 2019).

The 'differential' psychology that William Stern (1871–1938) founded at the turn of the 20th century was introduced by him as a *complement to*—not a substitute for—the general-experimental-individual psychology (Stern, 1900). Rather than focusing on common-to-all regularities in the psychological doings of individuals, the focus in this newly proposed sub-discipline would be on systematic *differences between* individuals in their psychological doings. The pursuit of that knowledge objective would require, by its very nature, an 'N = many' approach, and investigators would therefore have extensive use for just those aggregate statistical methods that were eschewed within the original general-experimental-individual psychology.

The epistemic implications of the shift from studies of *individual* psychological doings to studies of *individual differences* in psychological doings was not lost on William Stern. To the contrary, and though the matter was not a point of emphasis in his 1900 book, it was explicitly recognized in his second book on differential psychology, titled (in translation) *Methodological Foundations of Differential Psychology* and published in 1911 (Stern, 1911). In this latter work, Stern made clear his recognition of the logical fact that knowledge of the statistical properties of *variables* in terms of which individuals have been empirically differentiated from one another, i.e., knowledge of such parameters as the means, variances, and co-variances of those variables within populations, is not knowledge of the *individuals* who have been differentiated in terms of those variables. It is most unfortunate that this critically crucial insight of Stern's was obscured in the writings of other influential differential psychologists of his time.

For example, E. L. Thorndike (1874–1979) wrote in his book titled *Individuality* (coincidentally published in the same year as Stern's *Methodological Foundations of Differential Psychology*), that the correlation between two variables measuring between-person differences in two traits indicates "the extent to which the amount of one trait possessed *by an individual* is bound up with the amount *he* possesses of some other trait" (Thorndike, 1911, p. 22, emphasis added). This claim is simply false (see Lamiell, 1987, pp. 90–100; Lamiell, 2019, pp. 28–30).

Similarly, Hugo Münsterberg (1863–1916) wrote in his widely read paean to applied psychology titled *Psychology and Industrial Efficiency* (Münsterberg, 1913) that, given knowledge of the correlation between variables marking individual differences in distinct features of the psychological function of attention, "the manifestation of one feature ... allows us to *presuppose without further tests* that certain other features may be expected *in the particular individual*" (Münsterberg, 1913, p. 136, emphasis added). This claim, likewise, is false.

Altogether contrary to the stance taken by Stern (1911), the view projected in these quotations of Thorndike (1911) and of Münsterberg (1913) is that knowledge of variables in terms of which individuals are differentiated just *is*, at one and the same time, knowledge of the individuals who have been differentiated in terms of those variables. Moreover, it is this view, and not Stern's, that would be adopted by two of the most prominent of the next generation of differential psychologists.

The voluminous writings of Anne Anastasi (1908–2001) in differential psychology, beginning with the first edition of her highly influential textbook on the subject (Anastasi, 1937) and extending over many decades, give no recognition to the variables-individuals distinction drawn by Stern (1911). As a consequence, and quite unlike Stern, Anastasi (1937) viewed differential psychology not as a disciplinary complement to the general-experimental-individual psychology but rather as an investigative framework in which

... the fundamental questions are *no different* from those of general psychology. [For] it is apparent that if we can explain why individuals react differently from one another, we shall understand why each individual reacts as he does.

(Anastasi, 1937, p. vi, emphasis and brackets added)

In another widely read differential psychology text, the first edition of which appeared ten years after Anastasi's, Leona Tyler (1906–1993) confined her discussion of the historical roots of differential psychology to Stern's 1900 text (Tyler, 1947). As noted above, however, the variables-individuals distinction was not explicitly discussed by Stern in that text. By ignoring Stern's 1911 text, therefore, Tyler effectively blinded herself to that distinction, and so, if only by default, embraced the view of differential psychology shared by Münsterberg, Thorndike and, later, Anastasi.[2]

This, then, was the conceptual soil in the one of psychology's 'two disciplines' that Cronbach (1957) characterized as the "Holy Roman Empire" (p. 671) of 'correlational' (i.e., differential) psychology. In that soil, the view took firm root that statistical studies of individual differences can secure scientifically factual knowledge of the psychological functioning of individuals. Meanwhile, in the other of scientific psychology's 'two disciplines,' characterized by Cronbach (1957, p. 671) as the "Tight Little Island" of experimental psychology, developments were underway that would link it, epistemically, to correlational psychology. Knowledge claims in the two sub-disciplines would then be expressible in a common language.

Correlational studies of variables marking individual differences seemingly made differential psychology much better suited than the N = 1 framework for experimentation established by Wundt (refer above) for addressing practical problems arising outside of psychology's 'brass instrument' laboratories, e.g., in schools, business and industry, health care, and the military. As Münsterberg (1913) argued, a viable applied psychology would have to accommodate the reality—a reality avowedly outside the purview of the general-experimental-individual psychology—that "there are gifted and ungifted, intelligent and stupid, sensitive and obtuse, quick and slow, energetic and weak individuals" (Münsterberg, 1913, p. 10). However, a wholesale adoption of differential psychology's strictly correlational methods would undermine the discipline's suitability for discovering causal relationships (Danziger, 1990). That capacity was a strength of Leipzig-model experimentation, and was a feature widely considered essential to maintaining regard for psychology, both by psychologists themselves and by scientists in other disciplines, as a basic explanatory science and not merely as a kind of trade guild devoted to the production of statistical knowledge that could be put to practical use (cf. Wundt, 1913, 2013).

It was the availability of a form of experimentation that had been utilized for decades by medical researchers (Porter, 1986), treatment group experimentation, that seemed to obviate the need for psychologists to choose between the serviceability of correlational methods for the practical purposes of an applied psychology and the epistemic power of experimental methods for the scientific purposes of a basic psychology (Danziger, 1987, 1990). In the simplest form of such experimentation, groups of subjects are formed by assigning individuals at random to one of the two or more treatment conditions defining an independent variable (IV). A measure is then taken of the performance of each subject on some dependent variable (DV) used to represent ('operationally define') some or another psychological function. The findings of the experiment are then revealed by the outcome of a statistical comparison of the average DV values compiled by the subjects within each of the treatment groups. Where the difference(s) between those average DV values are greater than would be expected on the basis of random variation alone, it is concluded that the difference(s) are not the result of random variation alone, and it is inferred that the difference(s) reflect(s), at least in part, the causal effects of the differential treatments imposed upon the respective groups of subjects.

As experimental psychologists became ever more enamored with the treatment group approach to experimentation, the sub-discipline as a whole became ever better aligned with the work of the differential psychologists, as the work in both sub-disciplines was being devoted to statistical analyses of variables in terms of which individuals were being differentiated. The differential psychologists were using tests of one sort or another to statistically investigate correlational patterns in between-person differences that had arisen outside the laboratory. The experimental psychologists, for their part, were statistically investigating what were seen as the causal effects of between-person differences that they themselves were creating inside the laboratory. The statistical concepts and methods of investigation were the same across the two sub-disciplines (cf. Cohen, 1968; Kerlinger and Pedhazur, 1974), and, in both, the view prevailed that knowledge of the variables in terms of which individuals are differentiated—experimentally or otherwise—is, *de facto*, knowledge of the individuals who have been differentiated in terms of the variables. In the words of Danziger (1987), the ascendant interpretive custom was one according to which

> … the *statistical* structure of the *data* based on the responses of *many* individuals is assumed to conform to the *[psychological]* structure of the relevant *processes* operating on the *individual* level.
>
> (Danziger, 1987, p. 45, emphasis and brackets added)

Banicki: "Is the conceptual gap really so unbridgeable?"

Commenting critically on a recent article by the present author pointing out—yet again—the fundamental epistemic problem created by the conceptual gap between knowledge of variables defined only for populations and knowledge of the individuals differentiated from one another in terms of those variables (Lamiell, 2018a), Banicki (2018) subtitled a section of his text with the very question (which he posed rhetorically) in the heading above, and proceeded to defend his conviction that the correct answer to that question must be 'no.' He conceded the logical validity of the claim that the conceptual gap exists, but then dismissed the claim as "trivial" (p. 259) thanks to the long-standing convention of framing knowledge claims about individuals *probabilistically*. The same argument has been made in another recent article by Proctor and Xiong (2018; cf. Lamiell, 2018b, 2018c).[3]

The conceptual essence of probabilistic thinking as it is applied in this context is that knowing the proportion, P, of individuals within a population of size N who exhibit some phenomenon X under specified circumstances, one can validly infer that the probability is likewise P that, under those circumstances, an individual member of the designated population will exhibit X. In just this way, it is thought, one anchors the conceptual bridge that delivers one from knowledge of aggregates of individuals to grounds for valid claims to knowledge of the individuals within the aggregates. As an illustrative case, Banicki (2018) cited the findings of an experiment reported by Isen and Levin (1972), showing, as Banicki (2018) put it, that "people who had found a dime in a phone box were about 20 times more likely to help a stranger than those who had not been so lucky" (Banicki, 2018, p. 259).

In critically appraising this claim, it must be asked of Banicki's statement about "people" who found/did not find a dime in a phone box: *Which* people? Is the reference to each of 'this,' 'that,' and 'the other' person who found/did not find a dime? Is the reference to only some of them? In the latter case, which ones? And: how to know? Or is the reference actually to no particular person at all, but instead just to 'people' in the amorphous aggregate? Locutions of the sort used by Banicki (2018) are ubiquitous in the literature of mainstream psychology, and, routinely, the questions just posed are simply left to go begging.

Of immediate relevance to those questions is a basic logical reality discussed by the British polymath John Venn (1834–1923) over 130 years ago in his 1888 treatise of the concept of probability (Venn, 1888). Brought to bear on the Isen and Lewin (1972) experiment cited by Banicki (2018), that basic logical reality was that any given subject in that experiment either *would* or *would not* exhibit the target helping behavior. Just as surely as in a coin flip exercise like the one discussed for illustrative purposes by Venn (1888), where it is known in advance that any one flip of a fair coin will yield *either* a 'head' *or* a 'tail,' the 'would help/would not help' binary was the reality *for each and every one* of the individual subjects in the Isen and Lewin (1972) experiment, and this was true regardless of a given subject's experimental condition.

Banicki's (2018) '20 times more likely' claim is based on an empirical reality that Isen and Lewin (1972) documented by tallying up their 'helped/did not help' observations across subjects in each of the two groups into which they had been experimentally divided. One of those groups was composed of helpers who had found a dime; the other group was composed of helpers who had not. On the question of whether 'Smith,' who was observed to help, had been assigned to the 'found a dime' group or the 'did not find a dime' group, the experimental findings reported by Isen and Lewin (1972) and cited by Banicki (2018) are *completely silent,* and this is true for *every single subject* in the experiment. The '20 times more likely' reality was nothing that was or possibly could have been established for any individual subject. All of this just *means* that the findings of the Isen and Lewin (1972) experiment documented an empirical reality that was observed of, quite literally, *no one*. Knowledge of no one cannot possibly be knowledge of *any* living, breathing *someone.*

Unfortunately, mainstream research psychologists routinely take the ill-begotten liberty of discussing what their research reveals about 'people' in such a way as to imply an understanding of the term 'people' not as a reference to a *set* of individuals as a singular entity, but instead as a reference to a plurality of individuals each of whom is to be regarded as a distinct entity. Implicitly invoking just such an understanding, Banicki (2018) has effectively taken the findings of the Isen and Lewin (1972) experiment as scientific evidence that *a*—i.e., some given—individual person who has found a dime in a phone box would be "about 20 times more likely" to help a stranger than *a*—i.e., some other given—individual person who has not found a dime. Perhaps prepared to go even a step further, Banicki (2018) might possibly see the findings of the Isen and Lewin (1972) experiment as evidence that 'an' individual person who has found a dime would be "about 20 times more likely" to help a stranger than that same individual would be were no comparable serendipitous discovery made. From a scientific standpoint, the obvious problem with either of these individual-level interpretations is that neither conforms to what the Isen and Lewin (1972) experiment actually showed. With reference to any given individual, then, Banicki's (2018) '20 times more likely' statement cannot stand as a claim to *knowledge* about that individual. It could stand as an expression of Banicki's *subjective belief* about that individual, but it would have to be understood that that belief might or might not be confirmed by actual knowledge of what the individual does (or has done), and there is nothing in the findings reported by Isen and Lewin (1972) that establishes otherwise.

The larger lesson here is that no research findings of imperfect statistical relationships between variables marking between-person differences, whether as correlates of differences that have been assessed nonexperimentally by means of tests, or as effects of differences that have been created experimentally by alternative treatment conditions, can ever warrant claims to probabilistic knowledge about 'people' if 'people' is understood as a reference to distinct individual entities—i.e., *persons*—and not simply as a reference to unitary aggregates of such entities. This is why the only correct answer to the question posed rhetorically by Banicki (2018; refer above) is: 'Yes, the conceptual gap between knowledge of aggregates and knowledge of individuals within those aggregates really is unbridgeable.' Matters can be made to seem otherwise only by abandoning the frequentist understanding of probabilistic knowledge as tied inextricably to the consideration of a multiplicity of observations and embracing instead the subjectivist understanding of probabilistic statements as expressions of belief. Unfortunately, mainstream thinking in psychology has long systematically conflated these two understandings of probability (Cowles, 1989).

Nor should it be acceptable within a genuine science to maintain this indifference simply because doing so "appears to be working" (Banicki, 2018, 258). In the face of that notion, the question begs: *Working in what sense, and for whom?*

On the 'practical utility' defense of traditional mainstream interpretive practices

We can consider in this connection a hypothetical scenario constructed around the use of psychological tests as instruments for the pre-employment screening of job applicants (cf. Hogan, Hogan, and Roberts, 1996). In that scenario (cf. Lamiell, 2019), specialists in psychological testing who have been retained as consultants by a trucking firm have recommended that an individual, 'Lesley,' not receive further consideration for a job as truck driver. This recommendation has been based on (a) 'Lesley's' high score, X, on a test for the personality trait 'sociability,' and (b) statistical evidence, compiled through studies of large numbers of individuals, that highly sociable people have, on average, more accidents and hence are costlier to trucking firms, perhaps as a consequence of heightened distractibility, than are their less sociable counterparts. Clearly, exploiting knowledge of that aggregate statistical relationship in guiding employment decisions could facilitate the efforts of the trucking firm to minimize its operating costs in the long run. Doing this would also gain, for the consultants, compensation for acquiring and maintaining the technical expertise necessary in order to secure and then apply the requisite knowledge. In short, the practice of guiding employment decisions about individuals by the knowledge of statistical relationships discovered in studies of aggregates might, indeed, be said to be "working" to the financial advantage of both the employer and the consultants.

However: what about Lesley? She has been eliminated from further consideration for employment as a truck driver due to a high 'costliness' score predicted for her on the basis of (a) her high score on a test of the personality trait 'sociability' and (b) a population-level correlation between sociability scores and 'costliness.' Suppose that Lesley, or someone on her behalf, would inquire of the consultants about the accuracy of that prediction? If the consultants' answer to Lesley's question would maintain fidelity to the logical limits of the statistical knowledge on which the prediction about her has been based, the consultants would concede that although they could properly claim knowledge of *average* predictive inaccuracy across a large number of cases, they could not properly claim any knowledge at all of what the individual predictive inaccuracy might prove to be in Lesley's (or any other) particular case.[4]

In this light, it would be clear to Leslie that she, as an individual, had been eliminated from consideration for employment on the basis of a *prediction* about her future performance the accuracy of which was completely unknown! This would certainly give Lesley ample reason to conclude that the practice of basing employment decisions about individuals on the basis of aggregate statistical knowledge, a practice that might, indeed, be said to 'be working' very well for a business and for the consultants retained by that business, was not 'working' particularly well for her.[5]

Whether or not the interpretive practices of psychologists (and many other social scientists) may be regarded as 'working' despite their conceptual flaws depends greatly on whose interests are being taken into consideration. They will often prove to 'be working' very well for those whose interests are not with the affected individuals to begin with but are instead served best by minimizing their own predictive errors in the long run—i.e., on average, for a set or cohort of individuals. However, the same practices will often not be judged to 'be working' so well by affected individuals, whose interests are not encompassed by actuarial considerations (cf. Hanson, 1993).

From psychological science to psycho-demography and … back again?

As explained above, there is no viable conceptual bridge from aggregate statistical knowledge of variables with respect to which individuals have been differentiated to knowledge of any given individual among the differentiated, and this is true whether individuals are being differentiated by test scores reflecting differences that have arisen outside the investigative doings of researchers or by treatments that have created the differences inside the laboratory. Contrary to the hyperbolic claim of Hofstee (2007), this argument is not equivalent to "denying the right of existence" (p. 253) to research on between persons differences, whether correlational, experimental, or both. The argument does, however, force recognition of the fact that such research effectively constitutes a species of *demography* (Lamiell, 2018b; cf. Proctor and Xiong, 2018; Lamiell, 2018c). This is so because the knowledge generated by such studies is knowledge of *populations*, whether of real populations with a recognized existence quite apart from the projects of social scientists, or of hypothetical populations suggested by experimental treatments. The knowledge generated by such studies is not knowledge of *any* individual within those populations, but is, in fact and quite literally, knowledge of *no one*.

I have suggested that research of this sort be designated 'psycho-demography.' This term recognizes that the variables selected or created for investigation often reflect between-person differences in psychological attributes or processes, but still identifies the work as essentially demographic in nature. By no means is this designation intended as a challenge to the scientific merit or practical usefulness of well-executed studies of between-person differences in psychological attributes. For purposes of guiding public policy decisions, for example, psycho-demographic knowledge is often exactly the sort of knowledge that is needed. Moreover, the findings issuing from psycho-demographic studies can often prompt hypotheses about psychological processes that could be tested subsequently in studies that, unlike psycho-demographic studies themselves, are formally suited to the task of gaining scientific knowledge of the psychological doings of individuals (see chapter by Grice, Huntjens, and Johnson, this volume).[6]

In short, psycho-demography can serve hugely important practical functions in its own right, and it can also serve as a *complement* to a scientific psychology oriented to the advancement of our scientific understanding of the psychological doings of individuals. Widespread recognition of this would effectively re-align the two disciplines relative to one another as they originally were when William Stern founded differential psychology as a complement to the general-experimental-individual psychology pioneered by Wilhelm Wundt and others. This development, were it to transpire, would nurture a broader and deeper understanding among mainstream psychologists (and, perhaps, among social scientists more widely) of the true nature and limits of population-level statistical knowledge. In the process, conceptual space would be re-opened for a genuine psychology, one that is actually capable of advancing our scientific understanding of the psychological doings of individuals.

Notes

1 Hofstee (2007) has argued that this critique of conventional mainstream interpretive practices "counterfactually denies that people form expectations and make estimates, activities that are well represented by statistical models" (p. 253). The critique does nothing of the sort. The phenomena to which Hofstee (2007) referred are *psychological* in nature; features of the day-to-day cognitive functioning of lay persons well-documented in research conducted over many years by, most prominently, psychologists Amos Tversky (1937–1996) and Daniel Kahneman (b. 1934). The concern in the critiques that Hofstee (2007) cavalierly recommends be "taken with a grain of salt" (p. 253) concern the illogic of the reasoning reflected in the knowledge claims of trained scientists. The difference between these two concerns is apparent in the realization that there would be no grounds for labeling as 'biases' certain features of the day-to-day cognitive functioning of lay persons (cf. Tversky and Kahneman, 1974) were there no standard of logically sound reasoning against which to evaluate that functioning!

2 In an unpublished essay written much later in her career, titled *Neglected Insights in Personology*, Tyler (1984) clearly acknowledged that she had egregiously mischaracterized Stern's views (cf. Lamiell, 2003, pp. 1–2).

3 For a critical discussion of still another recent endorsement of this view, the reader is referred to pp. 222–225 of Lamiell and Martin (2017).

4 Were it otherwise, the consultants would simply correct their predictions by the putatively known error built into them, thereby eliminating their errors and making all of their predictions perfectly accurate!

5 Nor could the consultants validly finesse the issue here by claiming to know the 'probability' to be p that Lesley's 'costliness' score, were she to be hired, would be found to lie somewhere within the specified upper and lower limits of a so-called 'confidence interval' along the scale of 'costliness.' In this respect, all that the consultants could validly claim to know is that out of N cases with 'sociability' scores identical to Lesley's, $(p * N)$ of those cases would manifest 'costliness' scores falling within the designated interval and $((1 - p))*N$ would not. The question of which of those two groups would be found to contain *Lesley*'s 'costliness' score is a question on which the consultants' aggregate statistical data are completely *silent*.

6 For a detailed illustration of these points, see the discussion by Lamiell (2019, pp. 151–156) of work by Johnson, Markowitz, Hill, and Phillips (2016).

References

Anastasi, A. (1937). *Differential psychology: Individual and group differences in behavior.* New York: Macmillan.

Bakan, D. (1955). The general and the aggregate: A methodological distinction. *Perceptual and Motor Skills, 5*, 211–212.

Bakan, D. (1966). The test of significance in psychological research. *Psychological Bulletin, 66*, 423–437.

Banicki, K. (2018). Psychology, conceptual confusion, and disquieting situationism: Response to Lamiell. *Theory and Psychology, 28*, 255–260. doi: 10.1177/0959354318759609.

Cohen, J. (1968). Multiple regression as a general data analytic system. *Psychological Bulletin, 70*, 292–303.

Cowles, M. (1989). *Statistics in psychology: A historical perspective*. Hillsdale, NJ: Lawrence Erlbaum Associates.

Cronbach, L. J. (1957). The two disciplines of scientific psychology. *American Psychologist, 12*, 671–684.

Danziger, K. (1987). Statistical method and the historical development of research practice in American psychology. In L. Krueger, G. Gigerenzer, & M. S. Morgan (Eds.), *The probabilistic revolution, Vol. 2: Ideas in the sciences* (pp. 35–47). Cambridge, MA: MIT Press.

Danziger, K. (1990). *Constructing the subject: Historical origins of psychological research*. Cambridge: Cambridge University Press.

Grice, James W., Huntjens, R., & Johnson, H. (this volume). Persistent disregard for the inadequacies of null hypothesis significance testing and the viable alternative of observation-oriented modeling. In Lamiell, J. T., & Slaney, K. L. (Eds.), *Scientific psychology's problematic research practices and inertia: History, sources, and recommended solutions*. Abingdon-on-Thames: Routledge, forthcoming in 2021.

Hanson, F. A. (1993). *Testing testing: Social consequences of the examined life*. Berkeley: University of California Press.

Harré, R. (2006). *Key thinkers in psychology*. Thousand Oaks, CA: Sage Publications.

Hogan, R., Hogan, J., & Roberts, B. W. (1996). Personality measurement and employment decisions: Questions and answers. *American Psychologist, 51*, 469–477.

Hofstee, W. K. B. (2007). *Unbehagen* in individual differences—A review. *Journal of Individual Differences, 28*, 252–253. https://doi.org/10.1027/1614-0001.28.4.252.

Isen, A. M., & Levin, P. F. (1972). Effect of feeling good on helping: Cookies and kindness. *Journal of Personality and Social Psychology, 21*, 384–388.

Johnson, A. D., Markowitz, Al J., Hill, C. J., & Phillips, D. A. (2016). Variation in impacts of Tulsa pre-K on cognitive development in kindergarten: The role of instructional support. *Developmental Psychology, 52*, 2145–2158.

Kerlinger, F. N. (1979). *Behavioral research: A conceptual approach*. New York: Holt, Rinehart, & Winston.

Kerlinger, F. N. (1986). *Foundations of behavioral research*. 3rd edition. Chicago: Holt, Rinehart and Winston.

Kerlinger, F. N., & Pedhazur, E. J. (1974). *Multiple regression in behavioral research*. New York: Holt, Rinehart, and Winston.

Lamiell, J. T. (1981). Toward an idiothetic psychology of personality. *American Psychologist*, *36*, 276–289.

Lamiell, J. T. (1987). *The psychology of personality: An epistemological inquiry.* New York: Columbia University Press.

Lamiell, J. T. (1997). Individuals and the differences between them. In R. Hogan, J. A. Johnson & S. Briggs (Eds.), *Handbook of personality psychology* (pp. 117–141). New York: Academic Press.

Lamiell, J. T. (2003). *Beyond individual and group differences: Human individuality, scientific psychology, and William Stern's critical personalism.* Thousand Oaks, CA: Sage Publications.

Lamiell, J. T. (2015). Statistical thinking in psychological research: In quest of clarity through historical inquiry and conceptual analysis. In Martin, J., Sugarman, J., & Slaney, K. L. (Eds.), *The Wiley handbook of theoretical and philosophical psychology: Methods, approaches, and new directions for social sciences* (pp. 200–215). Hoboken, NJ: John Wiley & Sons.

Lamiell, J. T. (2016). On the concept of 'effects' in contemporary psychological experimentation: A case study in the need for conceptual clarity and discursive precision. In Harré, R., & Moghaddam, F. (Eds.), *Questioning causality: Scientific explorations of cause and consequence across social contexts* (pp. 83–102). Santa Barbara, CA: Praeger.

Lamiell, J. T. (2018a). On the concepts of character and personality: Correctly interpreting the statistical evidence putatively relevant to the disposition-situation debate. *Theory and Psychology*, *28*, 249–254. doi: 10.1177/09593 5431774837.

Lamiell, J. T. (2018b). From psychology to psycho-demography: How the adoption of population-level statistical methods transformed psychological science. *American Journal of Psychology*, *131*, 489–492.

Lamiell, J. T. (2018c). Rejoinder to Proctor and Xiong. *American Journal of Psychology*, *131*, 489–492.

Lamiell, J. T. (2019). *Psychology's misuse of statistics and persistent dismissal of its critics.* London: Palgrave Macmillan.

Lamiell, J. T., & Martin, J. (2017). The incorrigible science. In H. Macdonald, D. Goodman, & B. Decker (Eds.), *Dialogues at the edge of American psychological discourse: Critical and theoretical Perspectives in Psychology* (pp. 211–244). London: Palgrave-Macmillan.

Münsterberg, H. (1913). *Psychology and industrial efficiency.* Boston and New York: Houghton Mifflin.

Porter, T. M. (1986). *The rise of statistical thinking: 1820–1900.* Princeton, NJ: Princeton University Press.

Proctor, R. W., & Xiong, A. (2018). Adoption of population-level statistical methods did transform psychological science, but for the better: Commentary on Lamiell (2018). *American Journal of Psychology*, *131*, 483–487.

Stern, W. (1900). *Über Psychologie der individuellen Differenzen (Ideen zu einer "differentiellen Psychologie")* [On the psychology of individual differences (Toward a "differential psychology")]. Leipzig: Barth.

Stern, W. (1911). *Die Differentialle Psychologie in ihren methodischen Grundlagen* (Methodological foundations of differential psychology). Leipzig: Barth.

Thorndike, E. L. (1911). *Individuality*. New York: Houghton Mifflin.

Tversky, A., & Kahneman, D. (1974). Judgment under uncertainty: Heuristics and biases. *Science, 185*, 1124–1131.

Tyler, L. (1947). *The psychology of human differences*. New York: Appleton-Century-Crofts.

Tyler, L. (1984). *Some neglected insights in personology*. Unpublished manuscript, Eugene, OR.

Venn, J. (1888). *The logic of chance*. London and New York: Macmillan.

Wundt, W. (1912). *Elemente der Völkerpsychologie*. Leipzig: Alfred Kröner Verlag.

Wundt, W. (1913/2013). Psychology's struggle for existence (J. T. Lamiell, translator). *History of Psychology, 16*, 197–211. doi: 10.1037/a0032319.

3 Psychology's inertia

Epistemological and ethical implications

Fiona J. Hibberd

> *The undiscovered country ... makes us rather bear those ills we have,*
> *Than fly to others that we know not of?*
>
> Hamlet, act 3, scene 1.

In recent years, I have written two manuscripts which explained, with examples, how *conceptual* errors affect empirical research and render the "findings" misleading at best and false at worst. Both papers involved original research, aiming to address gaps in the published literature and both were submitted to appropriate mainstream journals, i.e., both complied with the journals' stated interests. Both received a number of desk rejections. The editors' reasons were occasionally implausible. The most common response was that I should submit my work to the *Journal of Theoretical and Philosophical Psychology*, even though I had been quite explicit about how empirical research would benefit from re-thinking the status quo. It would seem that the overriding obstacles to these manuscripts being sent out for review were that (i) they were *conceptual* research papers where no data had been collected and (ii) they addressed the discipline as a whole—they were not theoretical or methodological papers concerned with a specific empirical domain. I later rewrote one of the papers—on scientific definition—and, after minor amendments, it was published in a non-mainstream journal (Hibberd, 2019).[1]

More emblematic of this book's theme and far more egregious is the discipline's neglect of conceptual research *over many, many decades*. There are, for example, Joel Michell's many publications (e.g., Michell, 1986, 2020) which have yet to rehabilitate the mainstream's confused conception of measurement and its unshakable presumption that psychological attributes are measurable. And there are the critiques of operational definitions, from both outside psychology and within, which have consistently fallen on deaf ears for almost a century (e.g., Bickhard, 2001; Leahey, 1980; Russell, 1928; Waters & Pennington, 1938). I will return to these examples later.

Of course, the histories of other scientific disciplines can also provide examples of important research that was initially neglected. But psychology's disregard of conceptual research is chronic, systemic, and anti-scientific. It was evident during psychology's formative years, from the late 19th century until the 1940s, when so many moved uncritically into the behavioral and measurement paradigms, and has only become more entrenched since the post–World War II methodological consensus (Danziger, 1990; Gigerenzer, 1989; Lamiell, 2019).

Such disregard is, therefore, not best explained by the exponential growth of empirical publications which now exceeds our finite attentional resources (Thorngate, 1990), nor by today's neo-liberal university and its ever-increasing demand for "fast knowledge" at the expense of time spent thinking and exploring (Orr, 2002). These factors surely exacerbate psychology's reluctance to attend to conceptual matters, but a more potent influence was, and remains, late-19th-century positivism and its offshoots. Ernst Mach's (1838–1916) contributions were especially important (Danziger, 1979; Tolman, 1992; Winston, 2001). Diverging from Wundt, Mach denied the need for psychology to be exposed to any philosophical analysis.[2] As Blackmore (1972) attests:

> Mach's claim to not have a philosophy … was a major step toward accomplishing Auguste Comte's goal of persuading scientists to accept a positivistic philosophy while at the same time honestly believing that they held no philosophy at all, and that science—in particular their own special field—had successfully "advanced" beyond philosophy and the need to consider philosophical questions.
> (pp. 166–167)

Mach's positivism was to not only influence Karl Pearson, Edwin Boring, Edward Titchener, William James, and behaviorists such as B. F. Skinner (Blackmore, 1972; Smith, 1986), but also certain logical positivists who were subsequently appropriated by S. S. Stevens (1939) in his defense of a scientific psychology that admits only "… propositions based upon operations which are public and repeatable …" (p. 227). This endorsed an economical approach to science which aligned with American pragmatism (see Winston, 2001) and an ethos whereby anything that went beyond that which is given in experience was deemed not science. Empiricism was then refracted through this ethos and assimilated by psychology during those formative years. The result was a perverted form of empiricism, which "... (like the doctrine of the Trinity) it was more important to accept than to understand" (Toulmin & Leary, 1992, p. 607). Not everyone concurred with the positivist ethos, but most were content to amplify the message that for psychology to be a thoroughgoing, independent, empirical science, it had to be unshackled from philosophy and grounded solely in that which has been rigorously observed.

Notwithstanding the 20th–century refutations and demise of positivism and logical positivism, in psychology the positivist ethos persists. The Americanization of psychology's research methods across much of the world has meant that the discipline is now largely "... metatheoretically unreflective ..." (Mackay & Petocz, 2011, p. 19) and consists almost entirely of "... data-driven research and statistical presentation and assessment of results ..." (Ash, 2010, p. 20).[3] This has, according to critics, exacerbated its conceptual disunity and fragmentation. Psychology's accelerating empirical expansion has been characterized as fragmented bodies of knowledge-claims inferred from its myriad data sets and models that yield only "slivers" of theory relative to theories of any depth, breadth, or conceptual sophistication (e.g., Bickhard, 1992; Ceci & Williams, 2007; Koch, 1951; Machado & Silva, 2007; Robinson, 2000; Wachtel, 1980).

Unsurprisingly, critiques such as these have been largely ineffectual. They provide precisely the type of evidence that psychology so resolutely evades, *viz.*, sound argument without data collection that concerns the discipline as a whole.[4] In the sections that follow, I consider the epistemological and ethical consequences of this evasion, before turning to how the situation might best be redressed.

Psychology's defective concepts of method and evidence

The conventional wisdom in psychology is that scientific progress is achieved through the empirical testing of hypotheses which, given good quality observational data, permits the construction or refinement of a model or theory. Additional hypotheses can then be derived from that model or theory, these are tested empirically, and the sequence repeats. As a matter of course, this conventional wisdom is reflected in psychology's research practices, in textbooks about research in psychology, in what we teach and don't teach our students, and in the discipline's requirements for accreditation.

Yet, this conventional wisdom is flawed. It ignores the fact that the *conceptual* testing of theories, models, and all that is presupposed by them, is also a necessary condition of *scientific* research (Petocz &

Newbery, 2010). By *conceptual testing*, I mean that the statements which constitute psychology's theories, models and concepts are examined with the aim of uncovering vague, ambiguous, unjustified claims, internal inconsistencies, incoherencies, hidden implausible assumptions, and any other conceptual problem which *may indicate error or establish falsehood*. It also involves clarifying concepts, i.e., specifying the conditions for their legitimate use *without violating logic* (e.g., the logic of relations) and, where appropriate, reformulating statements in which the newly clarified concepts are embedded. There are excellent examples of conceptual testing—Bennett & Hacker's (2003) text on the *Philosophical Foundations of Neuroscience*, for instance—but, most of the time, this type of research escapes the notice of most psychologists.

Why is such research essential to scientific progress?[5] The phenomena investigated by any science have both *form* and *content*.[6] *Content* roughly demarcates one discipline from another. A psychological process, for example, consists of features or conditions not found in geoscience; such features are, then, discipline-specific. But other features or conditions are not. They are the *logical* (or formal) features common to *all* that exists and occurs in this world and are, therefore, "topicneutral" (Ryle, 1954). They have no lesser ontological status; they are just as real as discipline-specific features, but they are invariant across disciplinary domains.[7] It follows from their universality that *no data set could discriminate between occasions where these conditions do occur and occasions where they do not*. This means that conceptual problems cannot be solved by simply collecting more data.

Most importantly, logical (or formal) features run through all discipline-specific content; they are not separate from it.[8] For example, when psychologists contravene the condition that *no relation is internal to the items connected by that relation*, this logical error is *in* their scientific research.[9] It underpins the point originally made by Bakan (1955) and reiterated by Lamiell over many decades and in this volume—that psychologists illegitimately use mean differences between (sample estimates of) populations to say something about the *nature* of a particular condition that certain individuals are the bearers of. But differences between individuals (which are relational) cannot tell us about the individuals qua individuals because a difference relation cannot be an attribute of either individual, nor can it be a feature of the condition that an individual might be the bearer of. Bakan's and Lamiell's criticism is really of a formal kind, and they make the criticism because the logical conflation by psychologists amounts to a conceptual error that has implications for the selection of appropriate research methods which, in turn, determines the type of data collected.[10]

The point that has been so long lost, because of psychology's positivist ethos, is that psychologists can make two kinds of error in their empirical research. They can misrepresent the particular features of a phenomenon, its content, and they can misrepresent its universal features and make conceptual errors. Because the universal is not separate from the particular, because logic "runs through" discipline-specific content, conceptual errors will make discipline-specific content misleading, at the very least. It is not enough to have your empirical house in order. Hence Bunge and Ardila's (1987) pithy observation that: "… many experimentalists waste precious resources measuring features that have not been adequately conceptualized, thereby producing heaps of useless data" (p. 126).

On the other hand, conceptual research, if done well, can provide psychologists with the best conceptual material for their empirical work. It is a scientific "help," as Bennett and Hacker's (2003) more discriminating comments indicate:

> Conceptual confusions may be exhibited in different ways and at different points in the investigation. In some cases, the conceptual unclarity may affect neither the cogency of the questions nor the fruitfulness of the experiments, but only the understanding of the results of the experiments and their theoretical implications. … In other cases … misguided questions may well render research futile. … Rather differently, misconstrual of concepts and conceptual structures will sometimes produce research that is by no means futile, but that fails to show what it was designed to show.
>
> (p. 5)

Psychology's conception of method is defective because it neglects *conceptual* research as a necessary (but not sufficient) condition of science.

Psychology's concept of evidence—as that *which references data* or *that which rests on what is observed*—fares no better because, again, the logical or formal features that run through all discipline-specific content are not acknowledged. To labor the point above, logical features infuse psychology's networks of assumptions, explanatory hypotheses, theories and models, all of which play a crucial role in determining whether data are collected, the nature of the data, how they might be best collected, and the research conclusions drawn. It follows that restricting a concept of evidence to the collection of data is unjustifiable. Evidence is *whatever* speaks to a target statement being either true or false. The evidence from conceptual research can do just that. For instance, conceptual research tells us that McCrae and Costa's (2008, 2013) five-factor theory of personality cannot possibly be true because a number of its key statements are logically impossible (e.g., Boag, 2011).[11] The fact that this theory remains in place despite having been ruled out, exemplifies the discipline's disregard for conceptual evidence.

False scientific claims

All disciplines depend on a concept of truth—that what is stated is actually the case—and non-trivial truths typically require sound scholarship and valid method. However, psychologists have long been inculcated into two myths which have eroded those requirements. The first is that a rigorous scientific definition is an "operational definition"—a variable or concept must be defined in terms of the operations that facilitate knowledge of it (see Hibberd, 2019).[12] That piece of mythology is typically extended to associate an operational definition with psychological measurement. For instance: "… how the construct is measured can shape how we understand or define it" (Barker, Pistrang, & Elliott, 2016, p. 53). This takes us to the second myth—that measurement is the assignment of numerals to objects or events according to rule (see Michell, 1999).

A few of the many publications critical of operationism were cited earlier. The most telling refutation is that such definitions are not scientific because they involve a conceptual (logical) error. They confuse the variable or concept with the means (the activities/operations) by which that variable or concept is identified (Byerly & Lazara, 1973; Michell, 1990). It is the most telling objection because it makes clear that an operational definition is a logical impossibility. When the question "what kind of process, state, emotion, memory, behaviour, or disorder is X?" is answered either by a description of the activities that purportedly enable knowledge of X or by a description of the activities that bring X about, those descriptions cannot possibly be a description of X. In that respect they are false—they do not answer the scientific question "what is X?" or "what does concept X reference?". Neither can they serve to demarcate X from other related concepts.

Likewise, when X is *not* a quantitative attribute but psychologists claim to have measured X, such claims are also false. This is because "quantity" implies not only ordinal but also additive structure. Michell's research shows that (i) there is no evidence to suggest that psychological attributes have anything more than some kind of ordinal structure, (ii) ordinal structure does not entail additivity because it does not satisfy the axiom of continuity, and (iii) defining X is a pre-condition of any attempt to determine whether X is quantitative (see, for example,

Michell, 1990, 2008). With respect to this last point, Michell (2009) notes that:

> ... the scientific task of discovering [whether the attribute is quantitative] cannot be accomplished until testers are able to define the attribute to be assessed. ... Where this has not been done for any attribute, claims to measure it are vacuous because they are made not only in ignorance of what measurement means, but also in ignorance of the character of the attribute involved.
>
> (p. 122)

And so, the widespread conception that measuring a psychological concept will fashion how we define it, places the technical cart (of "measuring") in front of the ontological horse.[13]

I say "ontological" because a scientific definition references *what-it-is-to-be* that kind of thing. It describes what it is in virtue of that makes X, X, i.e., the characteristic(s) or feature(s) or condition(s) that X has necessarily. The formal requirements and implications of scientific definition are set out in Hibberd (2019), but of particular scientific importance is the distinction between those features or conditions that X has necessarily and those which accompany X but are not necessary.

Genuine scientific definitions are by no means absent from the psychology literature (e.g., Gigerenzer's [2017] definitions of the reiteration effect and hindsight bias). And it is possible to uncover what X is without knowing what the formal requirements of scientific definition are.[14] Reaching a scientific definition of X may be a difficult and messy process but the topic is foundational to research. Scientific definitions require precision for the integration and differentiation of concepts (Gigerenzer, 2017). It is, then, a matter of scientific literacy that psychologists understand the principles of scientific definition and the logical and methodological implications, lest they appropriate some other form of "definition" that they mistakenly judge to be acceptable. This was Stevens' (1946) error when he blended stipulation, operationism, and a version of formalism (from the logical positivists) to provide psychology with a definition of measurement that, to this day, remains widely accepted, despite the definition being false and incompatible with the traditional understanding of measurement (Michell, 1999).[15]

More will be said about psychology's uncritical acceptance of Stevens' concept of measurement in Hohn's chapter. Suffice it say here that, notwithstanding occasional fortuitous research outcomes, no science makes sustained, systematic advances through illegitimately defined concepts and misguided attempts at their measurement.

A failure at self-correction

An essential feature of science, as distinct from other forms of human endeavor, is that it is self-critical and self-correcting. It follows that when error-correction consistently fails to occur within a discipline, the discipline is not functioning scientifically. This is the case in psychology. Detached from the evidence that conceptual research can provide, psychology has yet to establish an adequate process of logical/conceptual error-correction. Hence the perpetuation of these errors across generations of psychologists.

It is not that psychology eschews error-correction as an essential feature of science. The problem is that it understands it only through the lens of positivism. Tellingly, a book chapter concerned to "make science better at self-correction" is entitled "The Empirical March" (Makel, 2016). Likewise, over the last decade we have seen various proposals to improve the replication of research procedures. These clearly aim to mitigate empirical errors, but given that conceptual errors are, at the very least, no less significant scientifically, psychology's mistake is to not ensure that a comprehensive system of error-correction (*of both kinds*—the empirical and the logical) is in place to redress our mistakes. When conceptual evidence is dismissed or restricted to a venue where it will not be seen by all relevant parties, not taken seriously, not shared by them, not examined critically, and not tested, the rational convergence of scientific opinion is thwarted.

Unethical conduct

Psychology's positivist ethos with its systemic conceptual neglect has been nourished by the supposed flourishing state of the discipline and by the corporate university's demands for "frontier research" at the expense of reflective inquiry.[16] Habit and inertia have triumphed.

> [This] ... makes it easier for us to continue to believe a proposition simply because we have always believed it. Hence, we may avoid doubting it by closing our mind to all contradictory evidence. ... We thus insulate ourselves from opinions or beliefs contrary to those which we have always held.
>
> (Cohen & Nagel, 1934, p. 193)

Psychology's ongoing insulation amounts to an ingrained *not wanting to know*. It is unethical because it is at odds with the disinterested truth-seeking which marks genuine inquiry (Haack, 1996).[17] The discipline's integrity is compromised by its warped conceptions of scientific method and evidence, the neglect of arguments hostile to its *modus operandi*, and the absence of conceptual error-correction. This can affect human lives. The discipline's failure to take seriously the conceptual error discussed on page 26 is instantiated in the pre-employment screening scenario discussed by Lamiell (2019, and this volume). This should bring home the fact that errors of logic are not abstract conceptual issues far removed from the quotidian stuff of life (note 8). They should matter to a discipline that purports to understand and care about people.

Ironically, the largest and most powerful "gatekeeper" in Anglo-American psychology, the American Psychological Association (APA), provides an "Ethics Code" which recognizes that "… psychologists' scientific and professional judgments and actions may affect the lives of others." It recommends that psychologists "… seek to promote accuracy, honesty, and truthfulness in the science, teaching, and practice of psychology …" (principle C); *take reasonable steps to correct significant errors* (section 8.10); base their judgments from assessments on information and techniques sufficient to substantiate their findings (section 9.01a); use assessment techniques that are appropriate in light of the research (section 9.02a), and rely on "appropriate psychometric procedures and current scientific knowledge …" (section 9.05) (www.apa.org/ethics/code).[18]

The situational irony lies in the APA's diligent efforts in advocating integrity while publishing material that implicates the contrary. For example, sections of the *APA Handbook of Research Methods in Psychology* (2012), *Methodological Issues and Strategies in Clinical Research* (2016), and the *APA Dictionary of Statistics and Research Methods* (2014) perpetuate the warped conceptions of scientific method, evidence, and self-correction that resulted from the distorting effects of the positivist ethos. The APA has not managed to consistently uphold its own epistemological values.

Solutions to the problem?

As Slaney's chapter envisages, there is nothing to suggest that, within orthodox psychology and among its gatekeepers, any change is forthcoming. If anything, the preference for data-driven research has only hardened in recent times. The onus is then on those who think that psychology is now so deeply out of kilter (weighed down by an ever-increasing number of ill-conceived research papers) to do more than simply continue as before.

One proposal is that those who are sufficiently concerned act collectively to publish a many authored paper, which explains how conceptual research is a scientific help to the rest of psychology. (I have in mind something like the Open Science Collaboration [2015], which reported on the poor reproducibility of some psychological research.) Such a paper should explain why the collection of high-quality data, analyzed using sophisticated statistical techniques, will not automatically spawn new concepts and better theories that also have practical relevance. Of course, the audience is unlikely to be receptive and the multiple authors would have to suspend their disagreements and focus on that which they do agree (note 5). It would be more difficult for psychology to ignore such a paper if it could be published in a leading mainstream journal, though this would perhaps require prior negotiation with the editorial board. A series of shorter follow-up papers could subsequently function rather like the Intergovernmental Panel on Climate Change updates—as annual or biannual notices explaining our latest, more specific concerns. Abstracts could simultaneously be sent to the editors of mainstream journals (as alerts), to the APA and equivalent organizations in other countries, and to responsible media outlets (e.g., *The Conversation*).

All of that *must* be followed by an education campaign which elaborates on the themes above. As Hohn and Tafreshi note in their chapters, education is essential in overcoming psychology's methodolatry. In universities and colleges, the compulsory teaching of applied statistics occurs *ad nauseam*, yet *how* to actively engage in conceptual research and *why* it is necessary for high-quality empirical research, is seldom a compulsory feature of a psychologist's or student's education.

Conclusion

When writing for *Theory & Psychology*'s 10th anniversary issue, Daniel Robinson (2000) pointed to journal editors and asked each to "… commit one page to critical and conceptual analysis for each page devoted to statistics and 'methodism' …" (p. 47). His request was not taken up. Despite the refutation of positivist philosophy of science, psychology enforces its positivist ethos and, without any sense of the incongruous, its philosophical prejudice remains a powerful disciplinary ideology. Is psychology's prejudice akin to Hamlet's contemplation of a fear of the afterlife—the "undiscovered country"? Perish the thought of an afterlife where data don't rule!

Still, psychology and its gatekeeping institutions are not beyond repair and a program designed to develop understanding could address its nescience regarding logic and conceptual research generally. Perhaps that program's overriding theme should appeal to the discipline's pragmatism: that *in the long run*, time can be saved, money can be saved, and the quality of psychology's research greatly enhanced if we expand what counts as legitimate research. To borrow from C. Wright Mills (1959): "The most economical way to state a problem is in such a way as to solve as much of it as possible by reasoning alone" (p. 206).

Notes

1 At the journal editor's request, I removed a section on the steps involved in developing a scientific definition, a section that had been intended as "a help" to readers.

2 See, for example, Wundt and Lamiell [trans.] (2013).

3 This is sometimes accompanied by an antipathy towards those not "toeing the party line." Wachtel (2007) notes that there are "… numerous stories of more theoretically inclined psychologists' work being dismissively described as 'think pieces' by tenure and promotion committees" (p. 49). And I have been advised to stop using the word "philosophy," that "conceptual research" is an oxymoron, and to change my method of research.

4 My reference to "psychology" includes the discipline's "gatekeepers"— institutions such as the American Psychological Association, the editors of mainstream journals, especially those on methods, the authors of its textbooks, especially those on methods (see Costa & Shimp, 2011), and any other body that purports to develop and cultivate the discipline's scientific literacy.

5 The reason I offer differs from those employing Wittgenstein's post-*Tractatus* approach to language and philosophy (cf. Hacker, 2010; Racine & Slaney, 2013). See Hibberd (2016) for my discussion of those differences which, I think, are minor relative to the points which unite us in our critique of psychology.

6 This form–content distinction has a very long history with roots in Aristotle's *Posterior Analytics*. It is also evident in Frege (1903) and Husserl (1973). "Form" should not be confused with the formalism of the early twentieth century, where certain statements were said to be devoid of empirical content. The latter was taken up by logical positivism but could not be worked through consistently, i.e., without recourse to content (e.g., Hibberd, 2005, pp. 109–100; Passmore, 1966, ch. 17).

7 If these formal or logical features were not features of reality, they would have to be applied to reality. How, then, could they be justified objectively? Why should we prefer one set of logical criteria over another if the criteria were not "out there"? Perhaps because one set is a better fit with reality? Yet, "a fit with reality" implies that the logical features are already present in the world. Furthermore, attempts to apply these criteria from "outside," in the *a priori* manner of Kant or the formal manner of Russell and Whitehead, or treating the criteria as conventions of discourse, à la logical positivism and

social constructionism, invariably leads to a form of dualism (between the empirical and non-empirical) and to self-refutation (Hibberd, 2005, ch. 5).

8 Which is why logic is neither abstract nor *aprioristic*, as is sometimes thought, and why the formal–content distinction is not dualistic. It is also why neither psychology nor any other discipline, nor life in general can be completely independent from philosophy.

9 The same error also lies at the heart of mental representationism (see Hibberd, 2014).

10 Confusing generality with aggregation also features in psychologists' confusion between scientific definition and classification (Hibberd, 2019).

11 If a statement is logically impossible, it is empirically and technically impossible.

12 Psychologists sometimes use "operational definition" to mean something else—operations or procedures that test for, bring about, or assess a concept, variable, or effect. This is not scientific definition either.

13 This exemplifies psychology's long history of making its methods front and center while neglecting ontology (Koch, 1959; Robinson, 1995, 2007) and corresponds to the logical positivist maxim that "the meaning of a proposition is the method of its verification" (Schlick, 1932/1979, p. 311).

14 In Hibberd (2019), I discuss Gigerenzer's use of the adjective "operational" despite his definitions being scientific.

15 The immense effect of Stevens' error brings to mind the very apt title of Toomela & Valsiner's (2010) book *Methodological thinking in psychology: 60 years gone astray?*

16 An effect of this is evident in the conversation switching of Gozli's (2019) colleagues, away from discussions about theoretical ideas to their preference for the type of empirical research that has the short-term, practical outcomes which will benefit their research careers. The number of papers published, the likely success of grant applications, and even the academic freedom to pursue trivial questions, were all evoked as justification for their preference.

17 This is not to imply that research findings which are true are necessarily ethical.

18 Similar principles and standards are promoted by corresponding organizations from other countries.

References

American Psychological Association. (2012). *APA handbook of research methods in psychology*. Washington, DC: American Psychological Association.

Ash, M. G. (2010). Psychology. In R. E. Backhouse & P. Fontaine (Eds.), *The History of the Social Sciences since 1945* (pp. 16–37). Cambridge: Cambridge University Press.

Bakan, D. (1955). The general and the aggregate: A methodological distinction. *Perceptual and Motor Skills*, 5, 211–212.

Barker, C., Pistrang, N., & Elliott, R. (2016). *Research methods in clinical psychology: An introduction for students and practitioners* (3rd ed.). Malden, MA: John Wiley & Sons.

Bennett, M. R., & Hacker, P. M. S. (2003). *Philosophical foundations of neuroscience*. Malden, MA: Blackwell.

Bickhard, M. H. (1992). Myths of science: Misconceptions of science in contemporary psychology. *Theory & Psychology*, *2*(3), 321–337.

Bickhard, M. H. (2001). The tragedy of operationalism. *Theory & Psychology*, *11*(1), 35–44.

Blackmore, J. T. (1972). *Ernst Mach. His work, life, and influence*. Berkeley: University of California Press.

Boag, S. (2011). Explanation in personality psychology: "Verbal magic" and the five-factor model. *Philosophical Psychology*, *24*(2), 223–243.

Bunge, M., & Ardila, R. (1987). *Philosophy of psychology*. New York: Springer Verlag.

Byerly, H. C., & Lazara, V. A. (1973). Realist foundations of measurement. *Philosophy of Science*, *40*(1), 10–28.

Ceci, S. J., & Williams, W. M. (2007). Paul Wachtel was ahead of his time. *Applied and Preventive Psychology*, *12*, 13–14.

Cohen, M., & Nagel, E. (1934). *An introduction to logic and scientific method*. London: Routledge & Kegan Paul.

Costa, R. E., & Shimp, C. P. (2011). Methods courses and texts in psychology: "Textbook science" and "tourist brochures." *Journal of Theoretical and Philosophical Psychology*, *31*(1), 25–43.

Danziger, K. (1979). The positivist repudiation of Wundt. *Journal of the History of the Behavioral Sciences*, *15*, 205–230.

Danziger, K. (1990). *Constructing the subject: Historical origins of psychological research*. Cambridge: Cambridge University Press.

Gigerenzer, G. (1989). *The empire of chance: How probability changed science and everyday life*. Cambridge: Cambridge University Press.

Gigerenzer, G. (2017). A theory integration program. *Decision*, *4*(3), 133–145.

Gozli, D. (2019). *Experimental psychology and human agency*. Cham, Switzerland: Springer.

Haack, S. (1996). Preposterism and its consequences. *Social Philosophy & Policy*, *13*(2), 296–315.

Hacker, P. M. S. (2010). *Human nature: The categorial framework*. Oxford: Wiley & Sons.

Hibberd, F. J. (2005). *Unfolding social constructionism*. New York: Springer.

Hibberd, F. J. (2014). The metaphysical basis of a process psychology. *Journal of Theoretical and Philosophical Psychology*, *34*(3), 161–186.

Hibberd, F. J. (2016). Is conceptual analysis only an inquiry into rules for the use of concepts? *Theory & Psychology*, *26*(6), 815–822. doi:10.1177/0959354316650047.

Hibberd, F. J. (2019). What is scientific definition? *Journal of Mind and Behavior*, *40*(1), 29–52.

Kazdin, A. E. (Ed.) (2016). *Methodological issues and strategies in clinical research*. Washington, DC: American Psychological Association.

Koch, S. (1951). Theoretical psychology, 1950: An overview. *Psychological Review, 58*(4), 298–299.

Koch, S. (1959). Epilogue. In S. Koch (Ed.), *Psychology: A study of a science* (Vol. III, pp. 729–783). New York: McGraw-Hill.

Lamiell, J. T. (2019). *Psychology's misuse of statistics and persistent dismissal of its critics*. London: Palgrave Macmillan.

Leahey, T. H. (1980). The myth of operationism. *The Journal of mind and Behavior, 1*(2), 127–143.

Machado, A., & Silva, F. J. (2007). Toward a richer view of the scientific method: The role of conceptual analysis. *American Psychologist, 62*(7), 671–681.

Mackay, N., & Petocz, A. (2011). Realism and the state of theory in psychology. In N. Mackay & A. Petocz (Eds.), *Realism and Psychology* (pp. 17–51). Leiden: Brill.

Makel, M. C. (2016). The empirical march: Making science better at self-correction. In A. E. Kazdin (Ed.), *Methodological Issues and Strategies in Clinical Research* (4th ed., pp. 597–605). Washington, DC: American Psychological Association.

McCrae, R. R., & Costa, P. T. (2008). The five-factor theory of personality. In O. P. John, R. W. Robins, & L. A. Pervin (Eds.), *Handbook of Personality: Theory and research* (pp. 159–181). New York: Guilford Press.

McCrae, R. R., & Costa, P. T. (2013). Introduction to the empirical and theoretical status of the five-factor model of personality traits. In T. A. Widiger & P. T. Costa (Eds.), *Personality disorders and the five-factor model of personality* (3rd ed., pp. 15–27). Washington, DC: American Psychological Association.

Michell, J. (1986). Measurement scales and statistics: A clash of paradigms. *Psychological Bulletin, 100*, 398–407.

Michell, J. (1990). *An introduction to the logic of psychological measurement*. Mahwah, NJ: Lawrence Erlbaum.

Michell, J. (1999). *Measurement in psychology: A critical history of a methodological concept*. Cambridge: Cambridge University Press.

Michell, J. (2008). Is psychometrics pathological science? *Measurement: Interdisciplinary research and perspective, 6*(1), 7–24.

Michell, J. (2009). Invalidity in validity. In R. W. Lissitz (Ed.), *The concept of validity: Revisions, new directions and applications* (pp. 111–133). Charlotte, NC: Information Age Publishing.

Michell, J. (2020). Thorndike's credo: Metaphysics in psychometrics. *Theory & Psychology, 30*(3), 309–328.

Open Science Collaboration. (2015). Estimating the reproducibility of psychological science. *Science, 349*(6251). doi:10.1126/science.aac4716.

Orr, D. (2002). *The nature of design: Ecology, culture, and human intention*. Oxford: Oxford University Press.

Passmore, J. (1966). *A hundred years of philosophy* (2nd ed.). London: Duckworth.

Petocz, A., & Newbery, G. (2010). On conceptual analysis as the primary qualitative approach to statistics education research in psychology. *Statistics Education Research Journal, 9*(2), 123–145.

Racine, T. P., & Slaney, K. L. (Eds.). (2013). *A Wittgensteinian perspective on the use of conceptual analysis in psychology*. New York: Palgrave Macmillan.

Robinson, D. N. (1995). *An intellectual history of psychology*. Wisconsin: University of Wisconsin Press.

Robinson, D. N. (2000). Paradigms and 'the myth of framework'. How science progresses. *Theory & Psychology, 10*(1), 39–47.

Robinson, D. N. (2007). Theoretical psychology. What is it and who needs it? *Theory & Psychology, 17*(2), 187–198.

Russell, L. J. (1928). Review of Bridgman's 'The logic of modern physics'. *Mind, 37*, 355–361.

Ryle, G. (1954). *Dilemmas*. Cambridge: Cambridge University Press.

Schlick, M. (1932/1979). Form and content: An introduction into philosophical thinking. In H. L. Mulder & B. F. B. van de Velde-Schlick (Eds.), *Moritz Schlick: Philosophical papers* (Vol. II, pp. 285–369). Dordrecht: D. Reidel.

Smith, L. D. (1986). *Behaviorism and logical positivism: A reassessment of the alliance*. Stanford: Stanford University Press.

Stevens, S. S. (1939). Psychology and the science of science. *Psychological Bulletin, 36*, 221–263.

Stevens, S. S. (1946). On the theory of scales of measurement. *Science, 103*, 667–680.

Thorngate, W. (1990). The economy of attention and the development of psychology. *Canadian Psychology, 31*(3), 2652–2270.

Tolman, C. W. (Ed.) (1992). *Positivism in psychology: Historical and contemporary problems*. New York: Springer Verlag.

Toomela, A., & Valsiner, J. (Eds.). (2010). *Methodological thinking in psychology: 60 years gone astray?* Charlotte, NC: Information Age Publishing.

Toulmin, S., & Leary, D. E. (1992). The cult of empiricism in Psychology and beyond. In S. Koch & D. E. Leary (Eds.), *A century of Psychology as science* (2nd ed., pp. 594–617). Washington, DC: American Psychological Association.

Wachtel, P. L. (1980). Investigation and its discontents: Some constraints on progress in psychological research. *American Psychologist, 35*, 399–408.

Wachtel, P. L. (2007). Response to commentaries. Consonances and controversies: Investigation and its discontents revisited. *Applied and Preventive Psychology, 12*, 47–49.

Waters, R. H., & Pennington, L. A. (1938). Operationism in psychology. *Psychological Review, 45*, 414–423.

Winston, A. S. (2001). Cause into function: Ernst Mach and the reconstruction of explanation in psychology. In C. D. Green, M. Shore, & T. Teo (Eds.), *The transformation of psychology: Influences of 19th-century philosophy, technology, and natural science* (pp. 107–131). Washington, DC: American Psychological Association.

Wright Mills, C. (1959). *The sociological imagination.* New York: Oxford University Press.

Wundt, W., & Lamiell, J. T., [Trans.]. (2013). Psychology's struggle for existence: Second edition, 1913. *History of Psychology, 16*(3), 197–211.

Zedeck, S. (Ed.) (2014). *APA dictionary of statistics and research methods.* Washington, DC: American Psychological Association.

4 Intransigence in mainstream thinking about psychological measurement

Richard E. Hohn

The concept of measurement is taken for granted by most psychologists. Many enter the discipline with the presupposition that psychology must be capable of measuring psychological attributes (e.g., intelligence, depression, psychopathy). It is easy to presume that measurement in psychology is without issue, controversy, or debate. After all, how could psychology become such a productive scientific discipline without the capability of measuring psychological things? Unfortunately, not much attention is given to fundamental issues of measurement and the rich history of psychological measurement is oftentimes given an uncritical treatment, and this is typically presented over only several pages within the early chapters of introductory psychometric methods books. What is often missing from these histories is a critical appraisal of whether the perceived advancements in measurement were justifiable in the first place. It is one approach to trace the path of psychological measurement from its origins to the present day, but it is a much different approach to question whether that path was a defensible one for psychology to take.

Although psychology is often regarded as a scientific discipline, the concept of measurement that has prevailed has developed into one that deviates from the concept of measurement in other scientific disciplines. Drawing largely from Michell's (1999) history of psychological measurement, the primary aim of this chapter is to outline the history of psychological measurement through a critical lens. In doing so, a number of 'missteps' in the history of psychological measurement are described, which, taken together, suggest that psychology has been incorrigible in dealing with measurement issues. A secondary aim of the chapter is to briefly outline a contemporary critique of psychological measurement offered by Michell (1997, 1999, 2000, 2003, 2011, 2013), as well as describe some aspects of recent measurement debates.

Misstep 1: The early psychophysicists

The birth of measurement in modern psychology is generally attributed to the early psychophysicists – among them G. T. Fechner, Hans Weber, and Hermann von Helmholtz – who were German scholars trained in the physical sciences. The moniker of "psychophysics" they fell under is a direct reflection of their research aims, as they sought to empirically and systematically study psychomotor and perceptual phenomena as an extension of their physical science research. Dominant in scientific thinking at the time of the early psychophysicists was a view referred to as Pythagoreanism, which posits that all attributes are quantitative and therefore measurable. Steeped in notions of Pythagoreanism emerged what Michell (1990, 1999, 2003, 2011) has called the "quantitative imperative," which is the idea that measurement is a necessary precondition of science. The assumption that psychological phenomena were measurable served as a natural starting point for the early psychophysicists, whose own perspectives accorded with Pythagoreanism and the quantitative imperative. It is unsurprising, then, that psychology's earliest proponents presumed it was a quantitative science from the outset. Their error, according to Michell (1999), was a failure in determining whether the psychological phenomena they sought to investigate were quantitative *prior* to their attempts at measuring them. The simplest form of Michell's argument is that the mere act of measuring something does not confirm that what is being measured is quantitative, at least with regard to classical definitions of what it means for an attribute to be "quantitative." As such, Michell (1999, 2000, 2003) asserts the empirical demonstration that a phenomenon is quantitative is a step that comes logically prior to the development of methods by which to measure it. To the contrary, the psychophysicists, through various methods, attempted to measure psychological phenomena without establishing whether they were measurable in the first place.

That the psychophysicists, namely Fechner, would make such an error is not altogether unreasonable, for a couple of reasons. First, Fechner did attempt to empirically demonstrate the relationships between physical stimuli (e.g., brightness of light) and the perception of sensory intensity. Fechner even hypothesized a logarithmic relationship between stimulus magnitude and the perceived intensity of the stimulus. However, while he employed methods that attempted demonstrate that the changes in perceived intensity were proportional the changes in stimulus magnitude (e.g., the method of just noticeable differences), such methods did not directly test whether such perceptual phenomena were in fact quantitative. Instead they relied on further untested assumptions that perceptions were quantitative. As Michell (1999) explains:

> In determining [just noticeable differences], it is differences between stimulus magnitudes and the judgments of subjects that are observed. The intensity of the subject's sensation is never observed by the experimenter. So conclusions about sensations can only validly be drawn from observations of [just noticeable differences] by invoking additional premises.
>
> (p. 82)[1]

Second, as described, the early psychophysicists were conducting their work within the scientific *Zeitgeist* of the time and their error was at least made in earnest. Nonetheless, the assumption that the domain of mental phenomena could be investigated using the same methods and principles as were used for physical phenomena represents psychology's first misstep towards measurement.

Misstep 2: Practicalism and mental testing

The influence of early psychophysicists on modern psychological measurement cannot be understated. Charles Spearman and James McKeen Cattell inherited the quantitative imperative from their psychophysical training in German universities. They maintained that view upon obtaining positions in England and America, respectively. It was within England and America that a confluence of factors further legitimized a quantitative approach to psychology. Precedence was set by the anthropometric research of Frances Galton, who, although not a psychologist, was the first to apply statistical techniques to presumed measures of mental abilities (e.g., exam scores) in 1869 (Galton, 1869). Another factor that legitimized psychological measurement was the difference in how science was valued among German, American, and English universities. Michell (1999) describes the German psychophysicists as practicing science under the "conception of disinterested inquiry," wherein there was "minimal relevance to the practical problems of the day" (p. 93). In contrast, many European and American psychologists embraced practicalism, a perspective in which the value of a scientific endeavour was thought to be, at least in part, reflected in the practical applications of its outcomes. Reinforcing the adoption of practicalism in America and England was the societal reward for embracing such views and applying them to the emerging field of the mental testing of intellectual abilities (e.g., intelligence). Mental tests found practical use in domains ranging from childhood education to military personnel placement. The confluence of these factors created a potently habitable environment for a movement in mental testing to take hold. Consequently, these factors lent a perception of legitimacy to early measurement practices that were not based on any empirical determination that psychological attributes were quantitative. That is, the measurement of mental abilities was useful, even if the measurements themselves were of questionable validity.

Spearman's (1904) development and application of factor analysis would be one of the earliest forces in the mental testing movement. Spearman's work broadened the scope of psychological measurement to extend beyond the psychophysical work of his predecessors and into the realm of assessing intellectual abilities. Yet, the grip of the mental testing movement was perhaps the firmest within American psychology (Crocker & Algina, 1986). A student of Cattell's, E. L. Thorndike, became the driving force behind the widespread uptake of psychological measurement in American universities with the 1904 publication of his book, *An Introduction to the Theory of Mental and Social Measurements*. Together, Cattell's and Thorndike's respective works on intelligence helped bring about the mass production of intelligence tests. Here we encounter a second historical misstep for psychological measurement: Not only was the entirety of psychological measurement to that point founded on the Pythagorean assumption that psychological attributes are inherently measurable, but this assumption was now supplemented by notions of practicalism and the societal rewards that widespread mental testing could offer. As a result, the presumption that psychology was indeed a quantitative science would be met with little noticeable resistance for at least two decades.

Misstep 3: Redefining measurement

It was not until the 1930s that psychological measurement encountered its first strong critique. It came as a result of deliberations by the Ferguson committee, a group formed by the British Association for the Advancement of Science, whose mandate was to "report upon the possibility of Quantitative Estimates of Sensory Events" (Ferguson, et al., 1940, p. 345). The committee included both psychophysicists and measurement theorists from the physical sciences. Michell (1999) notes a sharp intellectual imbalance between the two groups, describing the committee as comprised of "the big guns of a confident, intellectually dominant, Campbell camp, and the pea-shooters of an intellectually limp psychophysics camp" (p. 144). N. R. Campbell's (1920) theory of fundamental and derived measurement had found a strong foothold in physics at this time and while some aspects of his theory have been questioned, its core tenets remain the dominant view of physical measurement at present. Yet, Campbell's theory was largely ignored by American psychologists, as Campbell's theory of measurement was incompatible with the psychological attributes the psychophysicists on the committee sought to measure. This was primarily due to Campbell's criterion that fundamental measurement requires the empirical demonstration of an attribute's additive structure. This is most easily conceptualized when applied to some unit of measurement. For example, to represent the measurement of a rod as two centimetres, it must be empirically demonstrable that the rod's length could also be achieved by adding two smaller magnitudes together, say two lengths of one centimetre each. Thus, the numerical system in which two is double that of one directly reflects an additive empirical relationship of the magnitudes of the rod for which a rod measuring two centimetres must be double the physical magnitude of a rod measuring one centimetre. To most readers, this proposition is an exercise in common sense; however, for the psychophysicists of this time the criterion of demonstrable additivity threatened the validity of many of their measurement efforts which were not built upon the numerical representation of additive structures (Michell, 1999).

The challenges arising from Campbell's measurement theory put the psychophysicists in a precarious position. On the one hand, their discipline was founded as an extension of the physical sciences, and presumably, they sought a commensurate degree of scientific legitimacy for psychophysics. On the other hand, directly confronting Campbell's challenges would undermine their measurement paradigm as they had no means by which to empirically demonstrate that psychological attributes had additive structures. Rather than addressing Campbell's measurement theory head on, the psychophysicists on the Ferguson committee argued that the meaning of measurement should be relaxed to accommodate their measurement practices. It was not long before psychology redefined its concept of measurement in a fashion that evaded Campbell's challenges and accommodated both psychophysical and mental testing applications.

Psychology's new conception of measurement was proposed by S. S. Stevens (1946, 1951) and it was quite broad. In redefining measurement, Stevens (1946) avoided Campbell's rigid theoretical conditions relating to the use of a numerical systems to represent additive empirical relations and instead offered the definition of measurement as "the assignment of numerals to objects or events according to rules" (p. 667).

Under this definition, any instance in which a numerical system could be superimposed upon empirical relations is considered measurement of some form, including non-additive ordinal and nominal structures. This idea is well known today as Stevens' typology of measurement scales.

Interestingly, Stevens' definition suggests a contradiction. One would think that something as ostensibly revolutionary to a science as redefining measurement would engender some degree of resistance, debate, or critical response. Yet, as Michell (1999) explains, Stevens' reconceptualization was not particularly revolutionary. Conveniently, Stevens' definition is amenable to virtually all of psychological research and was readily embraced by mainstream psychology with little resistance. To a critical eye, it could be seen as suspicious that altering something as fundamental to a science as its measurement paradigm changed virtually nothing about its measurement practices. Instead, Stevens' definition supplied psychology with the licence it needed to maintain its course.

Other factors also played a role in the widespread adoption of Stevens' definition. Psychology had come to embrace operationalism in concurrence with the general rise of a positivistic philosophy of science that was sympathetic to operationalist views. Stevens' definition fit well within these perspectives. Although positivism and operationalism ultimately faded from prominence throughout the 1950s and 1960s, Stevens' definition has outlasted its philosophical origins and has continued to be embraced as the dominant conception of measurement in psychology through the present day.[2]

The widespread acceptance of Stevens' conception of measurement effectively ended the measurement debate in mainstream psychology, at least insofar as it removed measurement issues from the purview of everyday psychologists (Michell, 1999). Issues that may have suggested the measurement practices of psychology were questionable were thought to have been solved by Stevens. Evidence for this proposition abounds in introductory research methods textbooks. If one were to peruse such works, it is highly likely that Stevens' definition, or some variant of it, can be readily found (Aftanas & Solomon, 2018; Michell, 1997). Most often, Stevens' scales of measurement are presented as the primary, if not only, measurement framework in psychology (Aftanas & Solomon, 2018).

Misstep 4: "A revolution that never happened"

Although Stevens' conception of measurement has dominated psychology, it has not thwarted progress in measurement theory generally. As

Cliff (1992) recounts, "the middle 1960s were an exciting time in quantified psychology. Striking advances were occurring in two directions, and their combined effect seemed likely to free psychology from strictures that had impeded its progress as a psychological science" (p. 186). The advances Cliff was referring to are (a) the formulation of conjoint measurement theory (CMT; Luce & Tukey, 1964); and (b) the rise of computer-assisted psychometric techniques (i.e., latent variable modelling). Cliff's (1992) words are no exaggeration for those critical of Stevens' views. Michell's (1997, 1999, 2000, 2003) critique and, in most cases, the debates it motivated, revolve around the incorporation of CMT in psychological measurement in some form or fashion.

Unfortunately, a thorough exposition of CMT is beyond the scope of this chapter.[3] However, a concise explanation is warranted in order to express its potential value for psychological measurement. CMT is a formal axiomatic theory of continuous quantity, the application of which is purportedly able to quantify a set of variables (i.e., attributes) in circumstances in which direct empirical concatenation operations are not possible, such as when the variables are observed to be ordinal. As an axiomatic theory, CMT stipulates that if a number of formal statements are determined to be true as they apply to a set of related variables, the conclusion that additive structures underlie the variables can be deduced. According to Michell (1990), applying CMT can provide evidence for the additive structure of an attribute when measurements of some attribute are not *extensive*. Extensive measurement is a familiar concept to most, as the term 'extensive' is a reference to an attribute's extension in time and space. The earlier example using the concatenation of rods demonstrates this idea. The additivity of rods can be observed by their physical concatenation. For example, one can directly observe that the concatenation of two rods, each measuring one centimetre in length, yields a rod that measures two centimetres or double the length of unit defined as "centimetre" (1 cm + 1 cm = 2 cm). The additivity of psychological attributes cannot be tested in this way because they do not admit of spatio-temporal extension and therefore do not allow for observable concatenation operations (Michell, 1990).

In order to deduce the additive structures of a set of variables, those variables must first be established as comprising a *conjoint system*. Suppose that three ordinal variables, P, A, and X are related to each other. These variables comprise a conjoint system if they satisfy the following four criteria:

(a) P can possess an infinite range of values (e.g., reaction time);
(b) P is a function of A and X;

(c) *P* admits of ordinal structure;
(d) values of *A* and *X* are identifiable such that objects can be classified by their values (Michell, 1990, p. 69).

In cases where a conjoint system is observed, the set of variables is then subjected to four tests, each of which evaluates whether the relationship between the values of *P*, *A*, and *X* satisfy a unique CMT axiom. These axioms are referred to as (a) single cancellation; (b) double cancellation; (c) solvability; and (d) the Archimedean condition. If these axioms are satisfied, then it follows that *P*, *A*, and *X* are quantitative.

Importantly, CMT's axiomatic system is reminiscent of theories of physical measurement, so much so that extensive measurement can be shown to be a special case of conjoint measurement theory (Michell, 1990). Applying CMT, therefore, represents a potential solution to the challenges imposed on psychological measurement by Campbell and offers psychology an alternative to Stevens' operationalization of the measurement concept that more strongly accords with traditional scientific definitions of measurement. Beyond Luce and Tukey's (1964) introduction, CMT received an expansive treatment within three seminal volumes of *Foundations of Measurement* (FM; Krantz et al., 1971; Luce, Krantz, Suppes, & Tversky, 1990; Suppes, Krantz, Luce, & Tversky, 1989). It is discouraging, then, that as early as 1964 an alternative to Stevens' measurement concept was offered, but ultimately ignored. Telling is Cliff's (1992) thesis for his review of the FM volumes:

> My thesis is that, regrettably, the promise of the axiomatic measurement theory movement has not been fulfilled. Of the aspects of scientific psychology with which I am familiar, this work, at least as epitomized in the first volume of FM (Krantz, Luce, Suppes, & Tversky, 1971), is one of the highest intellectual achievements in psychology. Yet, one can argue that its influence on the mainstream of any aspect of quantified psychology has been minimal, in spite of the fact that its authors have in their own substantive work been among the most influential of scientific psychologists!
>
> (p. 187)

The failure to incorporate CMT into mainstream psychology represents a fourth misstep for psychological measurement. This misstep is compounded when one speculates upon the reason CMT was ignored. In the cases of the psychophysicists, mental test theorists, and Stevens himself, their missteps at least reflected their philosophical orientations of Pythagoreanism, practicalism, and operationalism, respectively. The rejection of CMT, however, came as a result of far less justifiable reasons. Research psychologists, understandably ill-trained in measurement theory, had a system that "worked," and it would take more than the esoteric treatises of a handful of measurement theorists to disrupt their traditions. To those measurement theorists sceptical of Stevens' definition, axiomatic measurement theory was thought to be a revolution (Cliff, 1992; Kyngdon, 2008a; Michell, 1999). Instead, it may well be a missed opportunity.

Misstep 5: Disregard of recent measurement debates

It has been shown that psychology's incorrigibility in the domain of measurement has been the result of several factors, among them psychology's maturation as a discipline (i.e., psychophysics, mental testing), response to meaningful criticism (i.e., the Ferguson committee, Stevens), and the discipline's disregard for theoretical progress. More recent measurement debates have involved critiques of current measurement concepts. This final section briefly examines the critique made by Joel Michell as well as some responses to it.

Michell: Psychometrics as a pathology of science

Michell (1997, 1999, 2000, 2003) has cast light on a history of uncritical measurement practices in psychology. Michell (1997, 1999, 2003, 2011) contends that psychology has long maintained the quantitative imperative, the view that the capability of measurement is a necessary precondition of scientific inquiry. Together with the Pythagorean notion that all attributes exist in some quantity and are therefore measurable, the quantitative imperative has driven psychology to adopt unjustified measurement practices in its efforts to "scientifically" investigate psychological phenomena, according to Michell's critique. Michell (1997, 1999, 2003, 2011) asserts that throughout its history psychology has failed to test the hypothesis that psychological attributes are quantitative, but instead has accepted as truth that such attributes are quantitative and therefore able to be measured *a priori*. As such because of the premise that psychological attributes are quantitative has been assumed to be true, psychology has conflated notions of psychological measurement with the development and application of psychometrics.

Michell (1997, 1999) describes the logical order for establishing a quantitative science as manifesting in two tasks: the scientific and instrumental tasks of quantification. *The scientific task of quantification* requires "the investigation of the hypothesis that the relevant attribute is quantitative," while the *instrumental task* consists of devising methods by which to measure magnitudes of the attribute if it has been demonstrated to be quantitative (Michell, 1997, p. 359). Psychology, according to Michell, appears to have reversed this logical order. It is for this reason that Michell (2000) has accused psychometrics of being a pathological science.

A science is considered pathological when it incurs a "two-level breakdown in processes of critical inquiry" wherein a hypothesis is first "accepted without serious attempts being made to test it" and second, the "first-level failure is ignored" (Michell, 2000, p. 639). The word 'pathology' is chosen carefully here to imply that psychometrics (and psychology broadly) has not made a mere error in neglecting to test the hypothesis that psychological attributes are quantitative. It is the *modus operandi* of science to support critical inquiry and, as such, errors are eventually realized and corrected in most instances (Michell, 2000). Rather, the history of psychological measurement demonstrates a *modus operandi* of deflecting critical inquiry (Michell, 1999, 2000). Without the invitation of critical inquiry mere errors either go unnoticed, or are dismissed *a priori*, and therefore no corrections can occur.

Continuing the measurement debate: Responses to Michell

Michell's critique may not have penetrated the mainstream of psychology, but his work has injected new life into the measurement debate. This is evidenced by an ongoing discussion that spans 20 years of publications in the journal *Theory & Psychology*. Numerous articles debating the theory and practices of psychological measurement have been published in the journal over that time, most of which address Michell's critique or issues it inspired. The remainder of this section is dedicated to outlining the primary counterargument to Michell, specifically, that item response theory (IRT) models, in particular the Rasch model, are probabilistic variants of conjoint measurement (e.g., Borsboom & Mellenbergh, 2004; Borsboom & Scholten, 2008). For ease of presentation, this section references only dichotomous IRT models, which apply to items with binary outcomes (e.g., yes/no, correct/incorrect).

IRT models are a family of probabilistic models that "[assume] item scores [on some psychological test] are a function of an underlying latent variable and uses this idea to formulate testable measurement models" (Borsboom & Mellenbergh, 2004, p. 108). Here we may take the 'latent variable' to be a statistical representation of some hypothesized psychological attribute (e.g., intelligence). IRT is unique compared to other psychometric approaches, in that IRT models estimate both continuous person parameters (i.e., participant estimates on the latent variable) and continuous item-level parameters, such as an index of the difficulty of an item and index of its capacity to discriminate participants across levels of the latent variable.[4] Ultimately, these item parameters define a logistic function, called an item characteristic curve, that maps the probability of correctly responding to an item (i.e., for a cognitive item) over the standardized continuum of the latent variable.

Proponents of IRT argue that these models can be thought of as probabilistic variants of conjoint measurement and that they are therefore are capable of satisfying the scientific task of quantification. Borsboom and Mellenbergh (2004) argue that, presented in its axiomatic form, CMT is too deterministic to suit psychological tests. For example, a deterministic model entails that if an estimate for a particular participant on the latent variable exceeds that of a particular item's difficulty parameter estimate, then the probability of the participant answering that item correctly should be equal to one. Likewise, if their estimate on the latent variable falls below an item's difficulty estimate, their probability of a correct response should equal zero for that item and one for all easier items. Viewing determinist models as too restrictive, Borsboom and Mellenbergh (2004) advocate for a probabilistic approach (i.e., IRT models) that can accommodate measurement error deterministic models do not allow for. Furthermore, they claim that the structure of IRT models is inherently additive, as the probability of a correct response is a function of the continuous person (i.e., participant estimates on the latent variable) and item parameters. These estimates might be thought of as reflecting a probabilistic conjoint system that can be subject to the adapted versions of the tests for additive structure specified by CMT. They further advance their argument by asserting that IRT models have strict assumptions that must be upheld, which, in conjunction with the tendency to reject models that do not fit well with their data, demonstrates that such methods do not accept hypotheses to be true without serious attempts to test them. That is, that such methods are not pathological.

Interestingly, the counterargument presented against Michell here is not sympathetic to Stevens' definition of measurement. In fact, Borsboom and colleagues' philosophical orientation is quite incompatible with Stevens' operationalism, as they claim proponents of IRT must "take a philosophically important step: they have to assume, *a priori*, that a latent trait exists, and underlies our observations, for otherwise they cannot construct a model that has testable consequences" (2004, p. 112). Their measurement theory, unlike Stevens,' does not shy away from ontological claims, but rather embraces one that is nakedly realist. Numerous other articles from this discussion investigate whether IRT models accord with CMT (e.g., Humphrey, 2013; Kyngdon 2008a, 2008b; Michell, 2014, 2017; Sijtsma, 2012; Sijtsma & Emons, 2013). I leave it to the reader to explore these arguments and draw their own conclusions. However, that contemporary measurement debates appear to have moved on from Stevens' measurement theory in favour of CMT is cause for optimism. Consequently, it further underscores the grave misstep mainstream psychology has made in the past by continuing to ignore the theoretical advances made towards measurement.

Michell was not the first to criticize psychology's approach to measurement, but his critique is the most substantial to appear in contemporary discussions of the subject and he remains an active contributor to the current measurement debate. Unfortunately, nothing has changed since Michell's critique confronted psychology's troubled methodological past. Stevens' operationalist concept of measurement remains cemented as psychology's primary approach to measurement. Of course, it may be the case that Michell's critique was considered and dismissed by the mainstream of psychology. More likely, however, is that Michell's critique has largely gone unnoticed outside of an insular group of psychological measurement theorists. Whatever the case may be, I contend that the lack of response to Michell's critique specifically, and the measurement debate more broadly, demonstrates another misstep towards a comprehensible psychological measurement. Either it confirms that psychology's *modus operandi* of dismissing criticisms is alive and well or suggests that the momentum of psychology's research enterprise is too great to allow for critical inquiry to receive attention in the first place.

Conclusion

This chapter has sought to outline psychology's troubled history of failing to confront challenges to its measurement paradigm. In doing so, a number of missteps in the history of psychological measurement have been described. As has been shown, psychology remains committed to a conceptualization of measurement that is impervious to critical appraisal. Several reasons may account for this, but it is most likely that psychology has had no practical incentive to deviate from its course. As Michell's critique has revealed, psychology has long embraced notions of Pythagoreanism, practicalism, and the quantitative imperative. Taken together, these views have encouraged the discipline to conflate the fundamental question of whether psychological attributes are quantitative with the act of devising ways to measure them (i.e., psychometrics). Most egregious is that when presented with a measurement theory that offered a potential avenue towards the axiomatic quantification of its attributes, the discipline balked. Instead, psychology has continued to advance Stevens' measurement theory as the only applicable theory within the discipline.

The implications of this are potentially far reaching. Significantly, psychology's current course undermines its claim to be a scientific discipline. Precise measurement is a fundamental component of a legitimate scientific endeavour, at least insofar as we take the meaning of science to be equivalent across the physical and social sciences. Should psychology wish to establish its status as a scientific discipline along these lines, it is necessary that it not selectively decide which tenets of science to adhere to. Psychology's reputation has already been questioned due to uncertainty in its methodological practices, including its mindless use of statistics (e.g., Cumming, 2012; Gigerenzer, 2004; Lamiell, 2019; see also Lamiell's chapter in this volume) and issues surrounding the replicability of psychological research findings (Open Science Collaboration, 2015). The adage 'garbage in, garbage out' is apt here, as these issues may never resolve if the measurements these practices rest upon are dubious or questionable. If valid measurement is the foundation of quantitative science, then psychology is at risk of someday seeing its foundation crumble beneath it.

Of course, institutional change comes slowly and incrementally, and one should not succumb to the illusion that psychology will reform its concept and practices of measurement with much alacrity. Although terms like revolution are routinely used in theoretical (e.g., Cliff, 1992; Michell, 1999) and philosophical contexts (e.g., Kuhn, 1962) one must remember that they still develop gradually as dissent of the accepted paradigm accumulates. The measurement debate in psychology represents one such slow-churning reformation, but its capacity to penetrate the mainstream of psychology has been historically limited. Put simply, the discussions within an insular group of measurement theorists are not enough. As such, those sympathetic to the issues presented here need to take it upon themselves to introduce the measurement controversy wherever possible, especially in teaching and instruction. I am under no illusion that comprehending measurement theory is an easy task, especially for beginning students, but that should not preclude the existence of a measurement controversy from being taught in psychological curriculums. Change can only come from the agents who make it, and the presentation of Stevens' definition, with no alternative, does not foster the kind critical thinking towards psychological measurement from which those agents might emerge. It is in part due to the lack of critical reflection of its measurement practices that psychology has found itself in such a precarious position.

Notes

1 Readers are directed to Michell (1999, ch. 4) for a detailed history of Fechner's measurement practices.
2 Readers are directed to chapters by Hibbard and Tafreshi, in this volume, for further elaboration of Stevens' conception of measurement.
3 For comprehensive treatments of CMT I direct the readers to Krantz, Luce, Suppes, and Tversky (1971), Luce and Tukey (1964), Michell (1990, ch. 4), and Michell (1999, ch. 4).
4 In this example, item difficulty is defined as the estimate of the latent variable at which probability of a dichotomous item being endorsed (i.e., answered "yes" or some equivalent) or correctly (i.e., for a cognitive item) is 50%.

References

Aftanas, M. S., & Solomon, J. (2018). Historical traces of a general measurement theory in psychology. *Review of General Psychology, 22*(3), 278–289. https://doi.org/10.1037/gpr0000143.

Bond, T. G., & Fox, C. M. (2001). *Applying the Rasch model: Fundamental measurement in the social sciences*. Mahwah, NJ: Erlbaum.

Borsboom, D., & Mellenbergh, G. J. (2004). Why psychometrics is not pathological. *Theory & Psychology, 14*(1), 105–120. https://doi.org/10.1177/0959354304040200.

Borsboom, D., & Scholten, A. Z. (2008). The Rasch model and conjoint measurement theory from the perspective of psychometrics. *Theory & Psychology, 18*(1), 111–117. https://doi.org/10.1177/0959354307086925.

Campbell, N. R. (1920). *Physics: The elements*. Cambridge: Cambridge University Press.

Cliff, N. (1992). Abstract measurement theory and the revolution that never happened. *Psychological Science, 3*(3), 186–190. https://doi.org/10.1111/j.1467-9280.1992.tb00024.x.

Crocker, L., & Algina, J. (1986). *Introduction to classical and modern test theory*. Fort Worth, TX: Harcourt Brace Javanovich.

Cumming, G. (2012). *Understanding the new statistics: Effect sizes, confidence intervals, and meta-analysis*. New York: Routledge.

Ferguson, A., Myers, C. S., Bartlett, R. J., Banister, H., Bartlett, F. C., Brown, W., ... Tucker, W. S. (1940). Quantitative estimates of sensory events: Final report of the committee appointed to consider and report upon the possibility of quantitative estimates of sensory events. *Advancement of Science, 1*, 331-349.

Galton, F. (1869). *Hereditary genius*. London: Macmillan.

Gigerenzer, G. (2004). Mindless statistics. *The Journal of Socio-Economics*, *33*(5), 587–606. https://doi.org/10.1016/j.socec.2004.09.033.

Humphry, S. M. (2013). A middle path between abandoning measurement and measurement theory. *Theory & Psychology*, *23*(6), 770–785. https://doi.org/10.1177/0959354313499638.

Krantz, D., Luce, D., Suppes, P., & Tversky, A. (1971). *Foundations of measurement: Additive and polynomial representations* (Vol. 1). New York: Academic Press.

Kuhn, T. S. (1962). *The structure of scientific revolutions*. Chicago: University of Chicago Press.

Kyngdon, A. (2008a). Conjoint measurement, error and the Rasch model. *Theory & Psychology*, *18*(1), 125–131. https://doi.org/10.1177/0959354307086927.

Kyngdon, A. (2008b). The Rasch model from the perspective of the representational theory of measurement. *Theory & Psychology*, *18*(1), 89–109. https://doi.org/10.1177/0959354307086924.

Lamiell, J. T. (2019). *Psychology's misuse of statistics and persistent dismissal of its critics*. Basingstoke: Palgrave Macmillan. https://doi.org/10.1007/978-3-030-12131-0.

Luce, R. D., Krantz, D. H., Suppes, P., & Tversky, A. (1990). *Foundations of measurement: Representation, axiomatization, and invariance* (Vol. 3). New York: Academic Press.

Luce, R. D., & Tukey, J. W. (1964). Simultaneous conjoint measurement: A new type of fundamental measurement. *Journal of Mathematical Psychology*, *1*(1), 1–27. https://doi.org/10.1016/0022-2496(64)90015-X.

Michell, J. (1990). *An introduction to the logic of psychological measurement*. Hillsdale, NJ: Lawrence Erlbaum Associates.

Michell, J. (1997). Quantitative science and the definition of measurement in psychology. *British Journal of Psychology*, *88*, 355–383. https://doi.org/10.1111/j.2044-8295.1997.tb02641.x.

Michell, J. (1999). *Measurement in psychology: A critical history of a methodological concept*. Cambridge: Cambridge University Press.

Michell, J. (2000). Normal science, pathological science and psychometrics. *Theory & Psychology*, *10*(5), 639–667. https://doi.org/10.1177/0959354300105004.

Michell, J. (2003). The quantitative imperative. *Theory & Psychology*, *13*(1), 5–31. https://doi.org/10.1177/0959354303013001758.

Michell, J. (2011). Qualitative research meets the ghost of Pythagoras. *Theory & Psychology*, *21*(2), 241–259. https://doi.org/10.1177/0959354310391351.

Michell, J. (2013). Constructs, inferences, and mental measurement. *New Ideas in Psychology*, *31*(1), 13–21. https://doi.org/10.1016/j.newideapsych.2011.02.004.

Michell, J. (2014). The Rasch paradox, conjoint measurement, and psychometrics: Response to Humphry and Sijtsma. *Theory & Psychology*, *24*(1), 111–123. https://doi.org/10.1177/0959354313517524.

Michell, J. (2017). On substandard substantive theory and axing axioms of measurement: A response to Humphry. *Theory and Psychology*, *27*(3), 419–425.

Open Science Collaboration. (2015). Estimating the reproducibility of psychological science. *Science*, *349*(6251), aac4716–aac4716. https://doi.org/10.1126/science.aac4716.

Scheiblechner, H. (1999). Additive conjoint isotonic probabilistic models. *Psychometrika*, *64*, 295–316. https://doi.org/10.1007/BF02294297.

Sijtsma, K. (2012). Psychological measurement between physics and statistics. *Theory & Psychology*, *22*(6), 786–809. https://doi.org/10.1177/0959354312454353.

Sijtsma, K., & Emons, W. H. M. (2013). Separating models, ideas, and data to avoid a paradox: Rejoinder to Humphry. *Theory & Psychology*, *23*(6), 786–796. https://doi.org/10.1177/0959354313503724.

Spearman, C. (1904). "General intelligence," objectively determined and measured. *The American Journal of Psychology*, *15*(2), 201–292. https://doi.org/10.2307/1412107.

Stevens, S. S. (1946). On the theory of scales of measurement. *Science*, *103*(2684), 667–680.

Stevens, S. S. (1951). *Handbook of experimental psychology*. New York: Wiley.

Suppes, P., Krantz, D. H., Luce, R. D., & Tversky, A. (1989). *Foundations of measurement: Geometrical, threshold and probabilistic representations* (Vol. 2). New York: Academic Press.

Thorndike, E. L. (1904). *An introduction to the theory of mental and social measurements*. New York: Science Press.

5   Persistent disregard for the inadequacies of null hypothesis significance testing and the viable alternative of observation-oriented modeling

James W. Grice, Rafaële Huntjens and Hailey Johnson

Perhaps nowhere is psychology's methodological incorrigibility more evident than in the realms of data conceptualization and analysis, particularly with regard to Null Hypothesis Significance Testing (NHST). Dating back at least 50 years, researchers, methodologists and statisticians alike have criticized NHST and implored psychologists to abandon it as their primary tool for drawing inductive inferences from their data (see Hubbard, 2016). No less of a figure than Paul Meehl famously wrote that NHST is "one of the worst things that ever happened in the history of psychology" (1978, p. 817). While not as dramatic as Meehl, the American Psychological Association formed a task force in the 1990s to address NHST's hegemony over research practice (Wilkinson & TFSI, 1999), but their attempts to encourage a more balanced approach toward data analysis that includes reporting effect sizes, confidence intervals, and visual presentations of data have largely been unsuccessful.

If there is safety in numbers, psychologists can rest in comfort knowing that other fields such as epidemiology, biology, education, and sociology have all developed an unhealthy reliance on NHST as well. It is perhaps this breadth of use and abuse, however, that finally drew the attention of the American Statistical Association (ASA) who released an official statement in 2016 urging researchers to curb their appetites for *p*-values (Wasserstein & Lazar, 2016). In October 2017 the international *Symposium on Statistical Inference* was then held and followed by a special issue of *The American Statistician* devoted to "a world beyond 'p < .05'" (Wasserstein, Schirm & Lazar, 2019). Somewhat anti-climatically, however, one of the primary recommendations of this latest effort was not a ban on the NHST paradigm itself, but rather a ban on the words "statistically significant." With 43 esoteric papers in the special issue that did not "sing as one" (Wasserstein, Schirm & Lazar, 2019; p. 1), it is hard to image this latest effort to get beyond NHST will prove any more successful than previous attempts.

A clue as to why failure is likely can be found in Hubbard, Haig, and Parsa's (2019) paper titled "On the limited role of formal statistical inference in scientific inference." As pointed out by these authors, the premise behind the special issue is that statistical inference is equal to scientific inference; however, the scope of the latter "transcends *by far* the purview of statistical inference" (p. 95, italics original). Stated more plainly, science is much older and much larger than statistics. One need only think of the remarkable scientific discoveries of Copernicus, Gilbert, Harvey, Darwin, Mendel, Newton, Einstein and countless others, all made without the aid of NHST, Bayesian statistics, or some variant thereof. To the extent psychologists continue to reduce scientific inference to statistical inference they will have no choice but to fixate on NHST and the multitude of ways to repair it or replace it with methods that accomplish the same, limited goal (viz., the estimation of population parameters from random samples).

From the standpoint of philosophical realism, scientific inference is tantamount to scientific explanation which is to understand some "entity, process, or property in light of its cause or causes" (Dougherty, 2013; p. 5). Because it is broader in scope while also requiring a deeper understanding of nature, scientific explanation is not something that can be neatly packaged into an algorithm or script that can be followed mechanically by a researcher. Learning to focus on scientific explanation instead of statistical inference will therefore require something of a Gestalt shift on behalf of modern researchers and their statistical advisers. Understandably, the prospect of such change will cause anxiety in today's competitive 'publish-or-perish' academic environment.

For their paper in the special issue, Hubbard, Haig, and Parsa (2019) sought to overcome this anxiety by advocating methods of establishing *significant sameness*. These methods incorporate familiar concepts and techniques such as significance, parameter estimation, and confidence intervals, but they are rightly considered as tools that can be employed in the larger quest for scientific explanation. The lesson here for those wishing to challenge the incorrigibility of psychologists and other researchers is that, reminiscent of Kuhn's (1970) "normal science," most academics prefer to work within the boundaries of a prescribed puzzle. Familiar concepts and techniques are regarded as most useful for filling in the gaps of the puzzle, while novel concepts and techniques are deemed perplexing and looked on with suspicion. Hubbard et al.'s *significant sameness* is rooted in the familiar territory of parameter estimation, yet it also opens new vistas by promoting philosophical realism and scientific explanation. Working with familiar concepts in order to nudge researchers out of their comfort zones may therefore be an effective strategy for overcoming the incorrigibility surrounding methods of statistical inference. In fact, this may be the *only* strategy when considering truly radical alternatives to NHST such Observation-Oriented Modeling (OOM).

First introduced by Grice in 2011 and rooted in the philosophical realism of Aristotle and Thomas Aquinas, OOM indeed encourages researchers to seek scientific explanations of natural phenomena. While statistical inferences may also be sought, they are not regarded as necessary for the development of scientific knowledge. Researchers are instead encouraged to diagram causal models that represent the entities, processes, or properties under study using all four of Aristotle's species of cause (material, formal, efficient, and final). These models are referred to as *integrated models* and they are the conceptual vehicles through which researchers both understand the natural world and through which they generalize beyond a given sample. Examples can be found in Grice (2011, 2015), Grice et al. (2012), Grice, Yepez et al., (2016) and Grice et al. (2017). In terms of data analysis, OOM challenges researchers to adopt an observation-centered (usually, this means a person-centered) attitude that eschews parameter estimation and even the computation of traditional statistics such as means, variances, and correlations. Instead, attention is directed toward assessing the accuracy of an integrated model as an explanation of patterns of observations. Confusing concepts such as Type I, Type II, Type III errors, and statistical power are also dispensed with, and the result is an approach to data conceptualization and analysis that is demanding and rigorous, but also straightforward and intuitive. A steady stream of papers has emerged demonstrating the efficacy of OOM while, following the strategy discussed above, also showing how psychologists and other scientists can deepen and extend their understanding of familiar concepts such as effect size, causality, measurement, and inference.

Effect size

With regard to effect size, numerous papers and book chapters have been written since the APA's task force on significance testing encouraged the computation and reporting of such statistics. In contrast to NHST, which is used to make inferences to population parameters from sample statistics, effect sizes are used to convey the magnitude of a given result. For instance, Diamond and Ravnskov (2015) reported data showing the relationship between statin consumption and coronary heart disease mortality. While the correlation was statistically significant at the liberal .10 level, it was extremely small in magnitude (viz., $r = .025$, $OR = 1.26$), thus raising questions about the efficacy of statins in reducing mortality. As this example demonstrates, effect sizes are considered to be more relevant than statistical significance to judgments of clinical, practical, or theoretical importance regarding a given finding. Today dozens of effect size statistics for quantifying group differences, variable associations, and relative risk are available to psychologists (e.g., see Kirk, 1996). OOM can be connected to these modern practices by providing researchers with the tools to answer the person-centered effect size question, "how many people in my study behaved or responded in a manner consistent with theoretical expectation?" For example, an OOM re-analysis of data from a recent study on the relationship between affect and perception showed that while the aggregate results yielded a statistically significant finding [repeated-measures ANOVA $F(2, 43) = 9.72$, $p < .001$, $\eta^2 = .31$], only 24.44% of the participants responded to the experimental tasks in a manner consistent with theoretical expectation (Grice et al., in press; Siegel et al., 2018). Grice et al. (2012), Grice (2015), and Grice et al. (2017) report additional OOM examples in which aggregate statistical analyses do not always provide a complete picture of one's results, consistent with Fisher, Medaglia and Jeronimus' (2018) recent reminder about the constant danger of the ecological fallacy. Moreover, as pointed out by Grice et al. (2017), hypotheses and theories are often framed in terms of individuals, yet most researchers nonetheless use aggregate statistics to analyze data. For instance, in their study of affect and perception, Siegel et al. theorized:

> Neuroscientific and behavioral studies suggest that affective feelings are integral to the brain's internal model and, thus, perception. The cytoarchitecture of limbic regions puts affective feelings at the top of the brain's predictive hierarchy, driving predictions throughout the brain as information cascades to primary sensory and motor regions.
>
> (2018, p. 496)

Clearly, the researchers were interested in a causal mechanism that operated within the common cytoarchitecture of each person of their study. They were not interested in an aggregated phenomenon, nor were they interested in some mythical "average person." Consistent with the tenets of philosophical realism, the goal of their study was to establish the existence of a general, causal mechanism underlying the patterns they hoped would emerge from their data.

Causality

Focusing on individuals paves the way for connecting OOM to statistical techniques used to make causal claims. Mediation models like the one shown in Figure 5.1 are particularly commonplace in modern journals. Such models can be quite complex, including multiple mediating and moderating variables as well as latent variables, and they provide the promise of offering evidence for causal claims without the necessity of performing randomized controlled experiments. OOM challenges researchers to consider two important questions when working with such models. First, what type of cause is being represented? Aristotle argued that to understand something in nature fully, its material, formal, efficient, and final causes must be explicated (Grice, 2014). As Collins, Graham and Flaherty (1998) have argued, mediation models are metaphorically similar to dominoes toppling one another in sequence and across time. If this metaphor is appropriate, then mediation models represent efficient causes. Second, how many people can be traced through a given mediation model? Causes are routinely understood to operate at the level of the person rather than in the aggregate. For the model in Figure 5.1, for instance, a parent grows distressed, which then impacts the child's self-attributions, which finally increases the child's depression. For this model it makes no sense to imagine the arithmetic mean of parental distress causally impacting the arithmetic mean of child attributions. Stated more bluntly and as a question, how can the average of parental distress, computed across different parents, cause the average of negative child attributions? Clearly, the causal powers are operating within the parent/child dyads in the study and not at the level of the aggregate.

The regression coefficients reported in Figure 5.1 were computed from data for 52 dyads. Using OOM, Grice et al. (2015) found that 24 (46%) of the parent/child dyads could be traced successfully through the mediation sequence: BSI → CASQ-R → CDI. A parent with high distress, for example, did not necessarily have a child with high negative attributions and high levels of depression. If mediation is like a series of dominoes toppling one another in time, then a parent with high distress should have a child with high negative attributions and high depression; or, a parent with low distress should have a child with few negative attributions and low depression. The observations

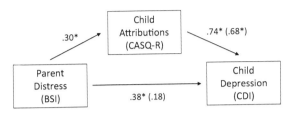

Figure 5.1 Path model for causes of childhood depression. Values represent standardized regression coefficients. BSI = Brief Symptom Inventory; CASQ-R = Children's Attributional Style Questionnaire–Revised; CDI = Child Depression Inventory. *p* < .05.

for a slight majority of the parent/child dyads did not match either of these patterns, thus failing to support the conclusion of "full mediation" reached through the traditional analyses. In another study of mediation, 54 women who had been raped were asked to rate their posttraumatic stress disorder (PTSD) symptoms, negative affect, and drinking behavior across 14 consecutive days (Cohn et al., 2014). The efficient cause (mediation) model, PTSD → Negative Affect → Drinking Behavior, was originally tested using Hierarchical Linear Modeling, and results revealed evidence for what methodologists refer to as "partial mediation." Using the methods of OOM, however, Grice et al. (2015) showed that only eight women could be accurately traced through the first link of the model, and only one woman could accurately be traced through both links in the model. These two examples therefore show that OOM provides the tools for researchers to offer a more complete picture of their results and to again avoid the ecological fallacy mentioned above. These examples also extend modern conceptualizations of cause by differentiating efficient causes from material, formal, and final causes. Grice (2015) and Grice et al. (2017) provide example studies incorporating formal and final causes, and they demonstrate how incorporating Aristotle's philosophy of causality provides a superior framework for modeling the complex structures and processes studied by psychologists.

Measurement

Attempting to trace individuals through mediation models will bring researchers face-to-face with the measurement problem in psychology, because to accomplish such a task they must work with the raw data ... with the observations themselves. For the second link in Figure 5.1 above, for example, each unit of observation (i.e., each possible score) on the CAS-Q must be matched with each unit of observation on the CDI; or, ranges of values must be matched. Linear modeling is avoided because it presupposes continuity of the attributes being studied. As Michell (2011) has strongly argued, however, there is no evidence that psychological attributes are structured as continuous quantities (see Hohn, this volume). Using the familiar language of Stevens' four scales of measurement, there is no evidence that the scores from the CASQ-R or CDI can be treated as interval or ratio scales, thus disqualifying standard linear regression as an appropriate method for analyzing these data.

An added benefit of working directly with observations is that important features of data are less likely to be missed. For example, what the mediation analyses above failed to reveal is that CDI scores were not normally nor uniformly distributed across the scale range (0 to 54); rather, 75% of the scores were ≤ 9, indicating low depression and raising concerns regarding causal claims drawn from these data. If the causes of depression are to be investigated, should not the sample contain a sizeable proportion of children with moderate and high depression? The issue here is one of range restriction, but not in the statistical sense, but rather in the sense of weakening a causal claim. As another example, Grice et al. (2020) reported a re-analysis of data from a study on male aggression in which an unusually high proportion of men (17%) showed no signs of aggression. This important feature of the data was missed entirely by the original regression analyses but detected by OOM because the observations themselves were analyzed.

The lack of valid units of measure for psychological attributes also adds support for the widespread use of nonparametric statistics. Using the familiar language of S. S. Stevens, these methods are designed for analyzing ordinal and categorical variables. The OOM approach provides a wide variety of tools that essentially mimic, complement or replace many nonparametric methods. For example, in a study of learning in honeybees, Grice, Craig and Abramson (2015) demonstrated how repeated-measures data can be analyzed using an Ordinal Pattern Analysis. In an experimental study on the factors contributing to individuals' attitudes toward controversial animal research, Grice et al. (2016) showed how logistic regression with continuous predictors can be replaced with purely discrete analyses. They also showed how logical combinations of observations can be constructed, such as the following statement that classified most participants (PCC = 73.02%) in the animal research study correctly:

Stop Research $\equiv$ (High Idealism $\wedge$ Female) $\vee$ (Low Relativism $\wedge$ Male)

In words, high idealism women or low relativism men were classified as desiring to stop the controversial animal research, whereas all other individuals were classified as desiring to continue the research. Finally, it is well known that nonparametric statistics generally rely on fewer assumptions than parametric statistics. In a study on laughter contagion among infants, Jordan and Thomas (2017) showed how radically skewed data, which violated important assumptions underlying the computation of p-values for repeated-measures ANOVA, could be fruitfully and validly analyzed using the methods of OOM.

Inference

With regard to inference, how does OOM compare to NHST and Bayesian estimation procedures? In order to answer this question, we here report a novel re-analysis of data published by Huntjens, Peters, Woertman, Bovenschen, Martin and Postma (2006). This analysis will also provide an opportunity to demonstrate some of the ideas and principles discussed above. In their research Huntjens et al. sought to understand the extent to which specific memories could be recalled under different identity states within individuals diagnosed with dissociative identity disorder (DID; formerly known as multiple personality disorder). For example, given two distinct identities within an individual, Robert and John, will Robert be able to recall information learned by John 30 minutes prior? The inability to remember or recall information across identity states is referred to as *inter-identity amnesia*, and its severity seems to extend beyond simple forgetfulness.

Nineteen persons diagnosed with dissociative identity disorder participated and first completed the Logical Memory (LM) and Visual Reproduction (VR) immediate recall tests from the Wechsler Memory Scale in one identity state. After 30 minutes they were asked to switch identities and were then given a multiple-choice recognition test consisting of 15 questions (10 for the LM, 5 for the VR). Total recognition, one of the primary dependent variables of the study, was computed by summing the number of correct answers to the recognition test. Three other groups of randomly assigned individuals also participated in the study. Persons in the simulation group (i.e., 'simulators,' $n = 25$) were instructed about the nature of DID one week prior to the study, and they were asked to create and practice switching to an alternate identity. For the study, these individuals followed the same protocol as the DID individuals, switching to their 'amnesiac' identities after 30 minutes for the recognition test. Persons in the control group (i.e., 'controls,' $n = 25$) also followed the same protocol as the DID individuals but were asked to complete the recognition task in routine fashion. Finally, persons in the guessing group (i.e., 'guessers,' $n = 25$) completed the recognition test without completing the prior LM and VR tasks.

Huntjens et al. analyzed the total recognition scores with a between-subjects ANOVA, $F(3,90) = 247.30$, $p < .01$, and pairwise comparisons showed the DID ($M = 3.11$) and simulators ($M = 1.88$) both scored significantly lower than the guessers ($M = 4.56$, p's $< .03$) and were themselves judged as statistically equivalent ($p < .09$). By reporting p-values and judging results as 'significant' or 'nonsignificant' Huntjens et al. used NHST (viz., H_0: $\mu_{DID} = \mu_{Simulators} = \mu_{Controls} = \mu_{Guessers}$) to draw inductive inferences to population parameters from their sample means. As shown by Lee, Lodewyckx and Wagenmakers (2015), Bayesian statistics can also be used to analyze these data, but despite their remarkable technical sophistication, the same type of inductive inference is sought. Both approaches to analyzing Huntjens et al.'s data also rely on key statistical assumptions, including random sampling and a continuous quantitative dependent variable.

There are several ways to analyze Huntjens et al.'s data using OOM. One approach is to compare each person in one group to every other person in a second group in reference to a hypothesized ordinal pattern (see Grice et al., 2020). Another approach that does not require specifying an *a priori* pattern, ordinal or otherwise, uses what Grice (2011) referred to as a binary Procrustes rotation algorithm. Adopting this approach, the results of the analysis that includes all four groups are presented in the *multigram* in Figure 5.2 (Panel A). As can be seen, the distributions of the four groups are presented side-by-side, and the bars are color-coded based on results from the rotation algorithm. Tallying the number of correctly classified individuals and converting to a percentage yields the Percent Correct Classifications (PCC) index, which for these data equals 74.47%.

Specific pairs of groups can similarly be analyzed while ignoring the remaining groups. As can be seen in Figure 5.3, when comparing the DID individuals to the simulators and guessers, the PCCs were equal to 75.00% and 79.55%, respectively, indicating the groups could be differentiated with some degree of accuracy. The DID individuals tended to score higher than the simulators and lower than the guessers.

64   *James W. Grice et al.*

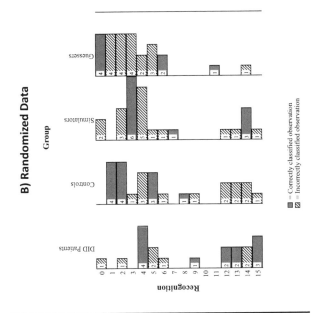

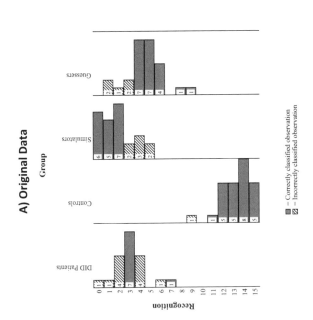

Figure 5.2 Multigrams showing classification results for four groups on the recognition task: (A) original data, and (B) randomized data.

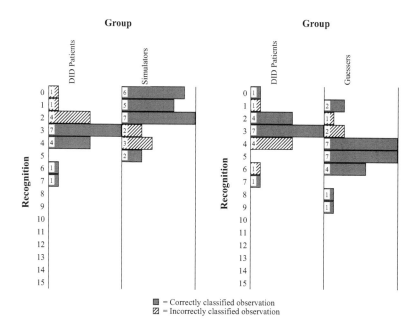

Figure 5.3 Multigrams showing classification results for specific comparisons of DID individuals to simulators and guessers.

NHST or Bayesian advocates may find the PCC index from these analyses to be interesting and useful, but they will likely wonder about its bias, consistency, and efficiency as an estimator of the corresponding population parameter. With OOM, however, the inference from a sample to a population parameter is of secondary concern or of no concern at all. Instead, each sample is regarded as a specific set of observations made through the senses under the guidance of a general, causal theory. Drawing an inference that terminates in choosing between two such causal (i.e., explanatory) theories of the same phenomenon is referred to as *inference to best explanation* (Mautner, 2005), and this is the inference sought when using OOM. In a study of memory, for instance, Grice et al. (2017) compared a classic mnemonic model of memory performance to a fitness-related (i.e., survival-based) model. When both models were compared to one another in reference to a single data set using OOM methods, the former model outperformed the latter in over 70% of the cases (PCC = 70.71%). For this one study and sample of data, the mnemonic model offered the best explanation of the patterns in the observations.

In many instances, however, researchers do not have two specific theoretical models to compare and are instead interested in evaluating a single theory or theoretical prediction. In such instances, can a researcher still seek an inference to best explanation? The answer to this question is 'yes' if one is both willing to consider chance as a competing model and to use a randomization test as part of the data analysis plan. As suggested long ago by Winch and Campbell, a randomization test can be used "to exclude the hypothesis of chance" (1969, p. 143) in route to a theoretically meaningful inference. In OOM a randomization test can specifically be used to evaluate an observed PCC in a way that is similar to computing a traditional *p*-value in NHST but without distributional assumptions and the assumption of random sampling. Moreover, hypotheses are not written in terms of population parameters, and cutpoints (e.g., alpha = .05) are not employed.

Returning to Huntjens et al.'s study, Figure 5.2 (Panel A) is compelling because the pattern of green bars indicates differences between groups that are theoretically meaningful. However, the pattern may simply be a chance occurrence, a fortunate intersection of various causal lines that are independent of inter-identity amnesia. A randomization test offers a method for determining how often such a pattern (or something even more compelling) would emerge if the observations were indeed paired by chance. Two competing inferences for Huntjens et al.'s data can now be compared:

I_1: The pattern of observations showing distinct clusters of total recognition scores across the four groups is best explained by the theoretical model of memory performance.

I_2: The pattern of observations is best explained as arbitrary pairings of the total recognition scores and group codes (i.e., the scores and codes are paired by chance)

As indicated by the second inference, the randomization test is conducted by randomly pairing the total recognition scores with the group membership observations. Figure 5.2 (Panel B) shows the multigram from one such randomization of the 94 participants, and as can be seen the original pattern has been degenerated substantially. The PCC of 43.62% for these randomly shuffled data is also over 30 percentage points below the PCC for the original data. This randomization process is repeated numerous times to generate a distribution of PCC indices to which the observed PCC can be compared. For Huntjens et al.'s data, 5000 randomized trials yielded a maximum PCC of 50.38%; therefore, not in a single instance was a randomized PCC equal to or greater than the observed PCC of 74.74%. This proportion is reported as a *c*-value (or *chance*-value), in this case $c < .0002$ since 1/5000 equals .0002, and it is used to assess the strength of the competing chance inference. The extremely low *c*-value here indicates the data cannot be easily shuffled to produce a PCC of at least 74.74%, thus supporting Huntjens et al.'s theory of memory performance as the more plausible inference to draw from these observations. The *c*-values (5,000 trials) for the specific comparisons shown in Figure 5.3 were .04 and .01, respectively, again supporting theoretical rather than chance explanations for the group differences on the recognition task. Contrary to the conclusions from the NHST and Bayesian analyses reported above, the DID persons are distinct from the simulators (PCC = 75.00%) and guessers (PCC = 79.55%) in ways not easily explained by chance.

What is lacking in this re-analysis of Huntjens et al.'s study is an integrated model that explicates the structures and processes underlying the group differences. Nonetheless, as the goal is to explain the patterns of observations, any published report of these findings would be centered round the multigrams in Figures 5.2 and 5.3. In terms of statistical values, the PCC would be treated as primary, and the *c*-value would be secondary. To aid readers familiar with randomization tests, the *c*-value can instead be reported as a *p*-value from a randomization test (e.g., randomization $p < .0002$, 5000 trials), and like any probability statistic it can never be considered as a substitute for replication. In addition to creating an integrated model, an important step forward in this research would therefore be an exact replication of Huntjens et al.'s study.

The methods demonstrated via this example also show that future data can be analyzed in a person-centered manner without computing a single mean, standard deviation or correlation, and without referring to an arbitrarily defined, imaginary population. Effect sizes as PCCs can similarly be person-centered, and the unrealistic measurement assumption of continuous quantitative structure entirely avoided. By streamlining analyses and escaping additional unrealistic assumptions associated with NHST (e.g., random sampling and distributional assumptions), intellectual resources are freed and can be directed toward the development of causal theories. Consequently, the long-term hope of extending our common conceptualizations of effect size, measurement, causality, and inference through OOM is that the theoretical horse will finally be placed in front of the methodological and statistical carts. In the parlance of Rychlak (1985), our metaphysics will no longer be ruled by our methods.

References

Cohn, A., Hagman, B. T., Moore, K., Mitchell, J., & Ehlke, S. (2014). Does negative affect mediate the relationship between daily PTSD symptoms and daily alcohol involvement in female rape victims? Evidence from 14 days of interactive voice response assessment. *Psychology of Addictive Behaviors, 28*, 114–126. doi:10.1037=a0035725.

Collins, L. M., Graham, J. W., & Flaherty, B. P. (1998). An alternative framework for defining mediation. *Multivariate Behavioral Research, 33*, 295–312. doi:10.1207=s15327906mbr3302_5.

Diamond, D. M. & Ravnskov, U. (2015). Additional commentary on deception in statin research. *Expert Review of Clinical Pharmacology, 10*(12), 1411–1412. DOI: 10.1586/17512433.2015.1102009.

Dougherty, J. (2013). *The nature of scientific explanation.* Washington, DC: Catholic University of America Press.

Fisher, A. J., Medaglia, J. D., & Jeronimus, B. F. (2018). Lack of group-to-individual generalizability is a threat to human subjects research. *Proceedings of the National Academy of Sciences, 115*(27), E6106–E6115. DOI: 10.1073/pnas.1711978115.

Grice, J. W. (2011). *Observation Oriented Modeling: Analysis of Cause in the Behavioral Sciences.* New York: Academic Press.

Grice, J. W. (2014). Observation Oriented Modeling: Preparing students for research in the 21st Century. *Innovative Teaching, 3*, 3. (27 pages) doi: 10.2466/05.08.IT.

Grice, J. W. (2015). From means and variances to patterns and persons. *Frontiers in Psychology,* 6:1007. doi: 10.3389/fpsyg.2015.01007.

Grice, J.W., Barrett, P., Cota, L., Felix, C., Taylor, Z., Garner, S., Medellin, E., & Vest, A. (2017). Four bad habits of modern psychologists. *Behavioral Sciences, 7(3)*, 1–21. doi:10.3390.

Grice J. W., Barrett P.T., Schlimgen L.A., Abramson C.I. (2012). Toward a brighter future for psychology as an observation oriented science. *Behavioral Sciences, 2(1)*, 1–22.

Grice, J. W., Cohn, A., Ramsey, R. R., & Chaney, J. M. (2015). On muddled reasoning and mediation modeling. *Basic and Applied Social Psychology, 37(4)*, 214–225.

Grice, J. W., Cota, L. D., Barrett, P. T., Wuensch, K. L., & Poteat, G. M. (2016). A simple and transparent alternative to logistic regression. *Advances in Social Sciences Research Journal, 3(7)*, 147–165. doi: 10.14738/assrj.37.2125.

Grice, J. W., Craig, D. A., & Abramson, C. I. (2015). A simple and transparent alternative to repeated measures ANOVA. *Sage Open,* July–Sept. 1–13. DOI: 10.1177/2158244015604192.

Grice, J. W., Medellin, E., Jones, I., Horvath, S., McDaniel, H., O'lansen, C., & Baker, M. (in press). Persons as Effect Sizes. *Advances in Methods and Practices in Psychological Science.*

Grice, J. W., Yepez, M., Wilson, N. L., & Shoda, Y. (2016). Observation Oriented Modeling: Going beyond 'is it all a matter of chance'? *Educational and Psychological Measurement.* doi: 10.1177/0013164416667985.

Jordan, E., & Thomas, D. (2017). Contagious positive affective responses to laughter in infancy. *Archives of Psychology, 1(2)*, Retrieved from https://archivesofpsychology.org/index.php/aop/article/view/18.

Kirk, R. E. (1996). Practical significance: A concept whose time has come. *Educational and Psychological Measurement, 56*(5), 746–759. DOI: 10.1177/0013164496056005002.

Hubbard, R. (2016). *Corrupt research: The case for reconceptualizing empirical management and social science.* Los Angeles, CA: Sage Publications.

Hubbard, R., Haig, B. D., & Parsa, R. A. (2019). The limited role of formal statistical inference in scientific inference. *The American Statistician, 73*, 91–98, DOI: 10.1080/00031305.2018.1464947.

Huntjens, R. J. C., Peters, M. L., Woertman, L., Bovenschen, L. M., Martin, R. C., & Postma, A. (2006). Inter-identity amnesia in dissociative identity disorder: A simulated memory impairment? *Psychological Medicine, 36*, 857–863.

Kuhn, T. (1970). *The structure of scientific revolutions* (2nd ed.). Chicago: University of Chicago Press.

Lee, M. D., Lodewyckx, T. & Wagenmakers, E. J. (2015). Three Bayesian analyses of memory deficits in patients with Dissociative Identity Disorder. In Raaijmakers, J.G.W., Criss, A.H., Goldstone, R.L., Nosofsky, R.M., & Steyvers, M. (eds.) *Cognitive modeling in perception and memory: A festschrift for Richard M. Shiffrin*, pp. 189–200. New York: Psychology Press.

Mautner, T. (2005). *The Penguin Dictionary of philosophy* (2nd ed.). London: Penguin Books.

Meehl, P. E. (1978). Theoretical risks and tabular asterisks: Sir Karl, Sir Ronlas, and the slow progress of soft psychology. *Journal of Consulting and Clinical Psychology, 46*, 806–834.

Michell, J. (2011). Qualitative research meets the ghost of Pythagoras. *Theory & Psychology, 21(2)*, 241–259.

Rychlak, J. (1985). *A philosophy of science for personality theory* (2nd ed.) Malabar, FL: Krieger.

Siegel, E. H., Wormwood, J. B., Quigley, K. S., & Barrett, L. F. (2018). Seeing what you feel: Affect drives visual perception of structurally neutral faces. *Psychological Science, 29*(4), 496–503. DOI: 10.1177/0956797617741718.

Stevens, S. S. (1946). On the theory of scales of measurement. *Science, 103*, 677–680.

Wasserstein, R., & Lazar, N. (2016). The ASA's statement on p-values: Context, process, and purpose, *The American Statistician, 70*, 129–133.

Wasserstein, R. L., Schirm, A. L., & Lazar, N. A. (2019). Moving to a World Beyond "p < 0.05", *The American Statistician, 73*:sup1, 1–19, DOI: 10.1080/00031305.2019.1583913.

Wilkinson, L. (1999). Task force on statistical inference: Statistical methods in psychology journals: Guidelines and explanations. *The American Psychologist, 54*, 594–604.

Winch, R., & Campbell, D. (1969). Proof? No. Evidence? Yes. The significance of tests of significance. *The American Sociologist, 4*, 140–143.

6   On the interpretative nature of quantitative methods and psychology's resistance to qualitative methods

Donna Tafreshi

As an educator of quantitative research methods, questions that I frequently receive from students include, "where does the alpha value come from?" and "how do I interpret the significance level?" There are, of course, answers to these questions that stem from convention. For example, I might respond to the first question by noting that, following from Fisher (1935), it has become convention in psychology to set alpha levels to .05 (but .01 and .001 are even better). However, a good student will further interrogate, "but why?" In fact, additional exploration into the question reveals that Fisher's interpretation of the "significance" concept was quite different from the one adopted under the common approach of Null Hypothesis Significance Testing (NHST) used today. Fisher (1935, 1956) did not intend .05 as a decision-making criterion, as he was opposed to such rigid criteria determining levels of significance. His interpretation was also different from that of his peers, Neyman and Pearson (1933), who proposed the concept of "alpha" on the basis of which decisions about a null hypothesis would be made, but who were opposed to such criteria being selected on the basis of convention. It is due at least partly to the hybridization of these two interpretations that we see conventional uses (or, some might argue, misuses) of the alpha concept under NHST today (see Gigerenzer, 2004; Lehmann, 1993).

The above example of how understandings of core concepts in NHST have been the topic of discussion and debate in statistical literature provides one illustration of how quantitative research methods are inherently interpretative activities. Yet, such activities are often taught to psychology students as if they are impervious to interpretation. As Gigerenzer (2004) noted, most statistics textbooks do not even mention the names Fisher, Neyman, or Pearson. What's more, there has historically been resistance to qualitative research methods in psychology (see Brinkmann, Jacobsen, & Kristiansen, 2014; Lamiell, 2019), which, in contrast to quantitative methods, are typically conceived of as being open to interpretation. This creates an illusion that research activities involving quantitative methods are fundamentally different from those involving qualitative methods due to the latter's interpretative nature. In the current chapter, I argue that if quantitative methods are taught in a way that emphasizes the interpretative role of tool users, similarities between the activities of quantitative and qualitative researchers become apparent. This, in turn, opens the door for the broadening of psychology's methodological toolbox.

Interpretation in qualitative research

It is widely acknowledged by qualitative research methodologists that a primary feature of qualitative research is an open reliance on interpretation as a meaning-making tool (see Denzin & Lincoln, 2005a; Willig, 2017). More than the mere distinction between numerical and non-numerical data, the interpretative features of qualitative methods stand out as a key characteristic of this domain of inquiry. Patton (2002) begins his introductory text to qualitative research methods by stating that "psychometricians try to measure *it*… statisticians count it… qualitative inquiries find meaning in it" (p. 1). The introductory chapter in the "Sage Handbook of Qualitative Research Methods" states, "qualitative researchers study things in their natural settings, attempting to make sense of, or interpret, phenomena in terms of the meanings people bring to them" (Denzin & Lincoln, 2005a, p. 3).

In their historical review, Brinkmann et al. (2014) emphasized several schools of thought that have been particularly influential for qualitative research, including hermeneutics, phenomenology, and pragmatism. Hermeneutics, or the study and art of interpretation, is traced to the works of scholars such as Schleiermacher (see Brinkmann et al., 2014) who focused on the interpretative nature of texts, and Heidegger (1927) and Gadamer (2013) who focused on the interpretative nature of human life. From a hermeneutic perspective, psychological and social worlds are, by nature, interpretative, and humans are, by nature, self-interpreting creatures. Next, phenomenology, originating in the works of Husserl (2008), posits that individuals make meaning of their lived experiences through engaging in an interpretative process that comes to constitute their knowledge of the world. Accordingly, the first-person accounts of individuals are central to understanding psychological phenomena. Lastly, under the tradition of pragmatism, most notably associated with James (1907), "truth" is viewed as being embedded in human action and circumstance. For a pragmatist, the goal of science is not necessarily to capture a fixed and objective reality but rather to understand reality in relation to one's actions and subjective experiences. There are, of course, other viewpoints that have been influential for qualitative research, including constructivism, feminism, and post-modernism, among others. The domain of qualitative research is not homogenous. For instance, a hermeneutic emphasis on meaning-making does not necessarily imply a constructivist epistemology. However, each of these perspectives attaches some degree of significance to human activity as interpretative. As such, the influence of hermeneutics, in particular, can be seen across the foundations of qualitative methodological approaches (see Brinkmann et al., 2014).

Interpretation is taken to be important to qualitative research partly because of the perceived complexity of qualitative data. Qualitative researchers typically discuss an interpretative analytic process through which one *makes meaning* from data. Moreover, a distinction is often made between *descriptive* analysis and *interpretative* analysis, the former involving mere recording of what is observed in data and the latter involving a creative process from which meaning is made from data (Patton, 2002). Although the procedural methods that encompass the various approaches to qualitative methods are diverse, some commonalities can be identified. Generally, qualitative analytical approaches proceed with the researcher first familiarizing herself with the data at hand (e.g., reading and re-reading text). This is followed by a "coding" process whereby notes that can be descriptive, interpretative, or both, are recorded, and an analytical process through which meaning is made from the data (e.g., Glaser & Strauss, 1967; Smith, Flowers, & Larkin, 2009). Of course, this is a very simplistic and generalized overview. However, the point I wish to emphasize is that open-ended interpretation is not only *explicitly acknowledged*, but also *encouraged* in qualitative research traditions. In fact, the entire analytical process is built on the notion that data are open to interpretation and that researchers, being self-reflecting and self-interpretive creatures, will interpret data with influence from their own lived experiences.

An emphasis on interpretation is taken to be an advantage of qualitative research over quantitative research. It is sometimes claimed by qualitative researchers that numbers do not answer "why" questions, that "measurement does not provide qualitative information of what is being measured" (Wertz et al., 2011, p. 4), and that qualitative research is much less rule-bound and less reliant on formulae to indicate "significance" of research findings (Patton, 2002). What is believed to tie together qualitative research methods, over and above the lack of reliance on numerical data, is a "loosely defined international interpretive community" (Denzin & Lincoln, 2005b, p. xiv). Qualitative researchers, despite their diverse epistemological positions, are all taken to be concerned with *meaning-making* in research (Willig, 2017). Quantitative research methods are perceived as being outside of the bounds of this community.

Interpretation in the activities of quantitative researchers

The American Psychological Association's (2012) "Guidelines for the Undergraduate Psychology Major" indicate that from early on in their education, students of psychology learning quantitative methods are expected to engage in interpretation. According to these guidelines, the act of interpretation in the context of learning quantitative methods is taken to be a fundamental aspect of information literacy. Students are expected to move beyond the technical language of statistics to interpret and explain findings using common everyday language. These guidelines further specify graphs, tables, statistical symbols, level of statistical significance, and effect sizes as the objects of these interpretative activities.

Although there is variation in the potential for different kinds of quantitative and statistical tools to be used in the analysis of psychological research (and the frameworks within which they are used), the teaching of quantitative analytical methods in North American psychology curricula is quite uniform. That is, if one were to examine various introductory statistics textbooks for psychological research, they would find familiar overarching structures and contents (e.g., Gravetter & Wallnau, 2013; Howell, 2010). Typically, texts begin with coverage of basic statistical concepts (e.g., variables), followed by a chapter or section on "measurement," and chapters devoted to descriptive statistics (e.g., measures of central tendency and variability), probability, and sampling distributions. Once NHST is introduced as an inferential device, the remainder of the book focuses on applying NHST to different research scenarios using various theoretical distributions (i.e., z-tests, t-tests, chi-square tests, F-tests). Here, I focus on examining the interpretative aspects of the major activities that arise from the above-described curricula, specifically, (a) applying psychological measurement principles to obtain data in numerical form; (b) conducting descriptive statistics; and (c) making statistical inferences, primarily in the context of Fisher's (1925) Analysis of Variance (ANOVA) and NHST.

Psychological measurement

Measurement in the field of psychology is conceptualized according to a definition that was presented by S. S. Stevens in 1946 under which measurement amounts to "the assignment of numerals to objects or events according to rules" (p. 677). Although this definition of measurement has been critiqued by scholars writing on the philosophy of measurement, it remains the most widely cited definition in psychology textbooks (see Hibberd, this volume; Hohn, this volume; Michell, 2004). As such, my focus here will be on Stevens' (1946) conception of measurement as a form of quantification or "pinning numbers on things" (Stevens, 1958, p. 384) and how it is applied in the field.

In presenting his definition, Stevens (1946) noted that numbers can be used to represent objects and events in different ways and according to different rules, and, because of this, one can define different scales of measurement that arise based on these varying rules: nominal, ordinal, interval, and ratio. The classic form of questionnaire scale that is germane to the field of psychology constitutes what would be considered an "ordinal scale." This involves ordered categories under which observations can be distinguished from one another based on rankings of those categories, but under which differences between ranks cannot be determined as equal. Although psychological research often also includes ratio scales under which a value of zero indicates an absence of the object being measured, such ratio scales are not germane to psychological phenomena; rather, they measure physical phenomena under the assumption that such phenomena provide information about psychological processes (e.g., reaction time, event related potentials). I will not be concerned with whether assumptions made about psychological phenomena based on physical measurements are warranted in this chapter; rather, I am concerned primarily with the activity of *psychological* measurement, namely, the assignment of numbers according to the principles of rank-ordering (i.e., ordinal scales).

Consider the case of Dr. Quantitative, a conventionally trained quantitative psychological researcher, employing the well-known Beck Depression Inventory (Beck, Ward, Mendelson, Mock, & Erbaugh, 1961). The BDI asks respondents to select a rating between 0 and 3 that best describes their current state for each of the 21 items in the questionnaire. For instance, ratings under item 1 correspond to the following descriptions: 0 = "I do not feel sad"; 1 = "I feel sad"; 2 = "I am sad all the time and I can't snap out of it"; 3 = "I am so sad and unhappy that I can't stand it." Prior to Dr. Quantitative being able to administer this scale to their research participants, some interpretation must have already been conducted in the development of the scale. That is, an interpretative process has taken place in which numbers have been tied to descriptive statements in a rank-ordered manner. Given that this is an ordinal scale, the numbers serve merely as labels that have been given the interpretation of ordered rankings. The label of 1 is interpreted as being greater than the label of 0, the label of 2 is interpreted as being greater than the label of 1, and so on. There is nothing *inherently* quantitative about the numerical labels themselves. Indeed, one could have chosen any variety of label to represent the different descriptive categories such as letters (a, b, c, d) or varying degrees of "sad faces." In other words, the *interpretation* of the *meanings* of these numerical labels is determined by the item writer. The interpretation is not inherent in the label itself.

What's more, the interpretations of the scale's numerical labels are *qualitative* in nature. A label of "0" indicates the qualitative and subjective experience of "I do not feel sad." The test creator had to have engaged in an interpretative process to determine that the subjective experience of not feeling sad can reasonably be taken as an adequate indicator of an individual's level of depression. That is, the test creator must have drawn from their understanding of the cultural and linguistic community within which the concepts of "sadness" and "depression" are used to interpret the meanings of these concepts as being tied to one another. Moreover, as a member of this same shared community, Dr. Quantitative is confident that upon reading the items in the inventory, they do indeed map onto shared meanings of "depression." Of course, Dr. Quantitative would also request information about the psychometric properties of the questionnaire (i.e., reliability and validity evidence); however, even with strong psychometric evidence, Dr. Quantitative would certainly question the legitimacy of the items if they had, for example, asked questions about whether someone loves Siberian tigers rather than if they feel sad (i.e., what psychometricians might refer to as "face validity"). Presumably, an affection for Siberian tigers is not closely tied to the concept of depression in the common discourse that the test creator and Dr. Quantitative share.

Alternatively, one might argue that the meanings of psychological scales are inherent in *data* obtained when the scales are implemented. Under this view, the meanings arise through the questionnaire administration process in which individual raw scores are obtained and compared with the scores of others. For example, part of this process might involve the establishment of standard scores or norms. However, Lamiell (2003) has shown that this conception is also false. While it is true that Dr. Quantitative might engage in a level of interpretation that discusses an individual's score in relation to other individuals' scores, the *meaning* of an *individual's* score cannot arise solely from such between-person comparisons. If this were the case, it would be impossible to place Dr. Quantitative's research participants on the scale until they were first compared with others. But such a comparison also cannot occur if other individuals had not already been placed on the scale. As such, Lamiell (2003) has illustrated that the meaning of an individual's score does not arise from between-person comparison but rather through active interpretation of the concepts implied by the scale such as, in this case, depression, sadness, etc. (see also Lamiell, this volume).

Thus, the act of developing items and analyzing "raw scores" on the BDI involves an interpretative practice of reflecting on the meaning of "depression." The interpretative item-response descriptions and their corresponding numeric labels become rules for the test-taker when they are tasked with selecting a response category for each item in the questionnaire. Upon receiving the questionnaire, the test-taker must interpret the statements, the scale (based on the rules laid out by the test creator/administrator), and most importantly, they must also interpret their own experiences in order to choose a response. That is, they must engage in a self-reflective and interpretative process that draws on their first-person subjective experiences.

Descriptive statistics

Whereas qualitative methods manuals tend to create a distinction between *descriptive* and *interpretative* analysis, statistical analysis manuals create a distinction between *descriptive* and *inferential* statistics. The latter distinction, however, does not rest on a separation between non-interpretative and interpretative activities. Instead, it can be shown that both the activities of descriptive and inferential statistics are interpretative by nature. The expression "descriptive statistics" refers to the analysis of data in which the primary aim is to describe a sample or subset of a population of scores. It is contrasted with "inferential statistics," the aim of which is to use statistics computed on raw sample data to make inferences about population parameters. Despite the fact that descriptive statistics is most commonly practiced in psychology as a transitory stage of analysis ultimately leading to inference, it is, in fact, a large area of inquiry that involves a variety of flexible analytical tools with the potential to construct powerful stories about observed data (see Tukey, 1977).

There are several layers of interpretation involved in uses of descriptive statistics in psychology. First, being that statistics is a technically constrained and highly rule-bound normative language, interpretation of data are also constrained by the rules of this language. For example, the concept of the "mean," perhaps the most popular descriptive statistic, is constrained to the technical interpretation of the "average value" and mathematically defined as:

$$\sum_{i=1}^{N} \frac{X_i}{N}$$

In words, the mean is the sum of scores on variable X divided by the total number of observations on X. If our researcher, Dr. Quantitative, calculated the mean total score for a sample of $N = 65$ respondents on the BDI as being equal to 23, they would be constrained by the language of statistics to interpreting this value as the "average score." It is, simply put, the sum of scores on the BDI divided by the total number of observations on the BDI.

However, the *meaning* of the mean is not as simple when it is applied in research practice through the activities of persons connected to a social and historical context. In 1832, Belgian astronomer and mathematician Adolphe Quetelet published "Sur l'homme et le développement de ses facultés, ou essai de physique sociale" (translated in 1842 as "A treatise on man and the development of his faculties") in which he presented aggregate level statistical analyses of birth rates, death rates, weights, heights, and other population characteristics. It is in this book that Quetelet's well-known conception of the mean as "l'homme moyen" or "the average man" was outlined. He explained, "if an individual at any given epoch of society possessed all the qualities of the average man, he would represent all that is great, good, or beautiful" (Quetelet, 1842, p. 100). According to Quetelet (1842), the mean was an ideal representation of society and deviations of individual scores from the mean, or "errors," represented flaws of society. As such, mediocrity was the ideal, and Quetelet (1842) argued that if one could examine a large enough group of individual characteristics, they would always obtain a normal distribution curve, confirming that the error law governed the activities of human societies. Quetelet was well aware of the technical definition of the mean as the average value in statistics, but it was his beliefs about humans and the laws of nature that influenced his interpretations of the *meaning* of the mean. As Porter (1986) aptly described, Quetelet's interpretation of the mean was representative of his moral values, chiefly, the idea that a life of moderation would lead to a prosperous society.

Quetelet's interpretation of "l'homme moyen" is largely rejected by scholars today. Whereas Quetelet viewed deviations from the mean as flaws of society, our modern Dr. Quantitative would view such deviations as variation, either due to individual differences or to random error, depending on the level of analysis applied. Like Quetelet,

Dr. Quantitative must grapple with her own interpretation of the mean. Upon conducting statistical analyses, she must determine what exactly it *means* for the study of depression that the mean score for the sample of $N = 63$ respondents on the BDI is equal to 23. What is the research *story*? This requires that Dr. Quantitative connect her summary statistics to the *meanings* of the numbers summarized based on her conceptual understanding of the BDI's qualitative scale labels.

Statistical inference

Dr. Quantitative's final stage of analysis will involve an inference made to the population mean of BDI scores based on the calculated sample mean. Here, Dr. Quantitative will be faced with the question of whether the mean BDI score observed is "significant." This question stems from the widespread use of NHST as an inferential tool in the field of psychology. Historically, the gold standard of inference has been NHST, while the gold standard of method has been experimental design conceptualized under the ANOVA framework proposed by Ronald A. Fisher (1925). In this section, I begin by examining interpretations of the mean and variation under the ANOVA framework before discussing the question of "significance" plaguing Dr. Quantitative in her inferential pursuits.

As mentioned above, although both Quetelet and Dr. Quantitative are interested in calculating means computed based on observations collected from different individuals, their interpretations of those means and deviations from them differ. Dr. Quantitative's interpretation stems from Fisher's method of ANOVA popularized through his seminal 1925 book, "Statistical Methods for Research Workers." In this book, Fisher (1925) defined deviations between scores collected from differing individuals/objects and a central value computed based on those scores (e.g., the mean) as "variation." He further explained that statistics is a field that is concerned primarily with studying such variation and making inferences to aggregates of individuals/objects based on those variations (Fisher, 1925). Fisher's focus on variations from the mean rather than on the mean itself was not a new proposal. He drew influence from the works of other statisticians such as Francis Galton (1869). Galton (1869) was familiar with and influenced by Quetelet's (1842) studies with the error law. However, unlike Quetelet, Galton did not believe that the error distribution curve represented an idealistic value at the center of society's flaws (Porter, 1986). Instead, Galton was interested in deviations of scores collected from differing individuals from the mean of those scores because he interpreted them as representing human variation (Porter, 1986). According to Galton (1869), such variation was truly a meaningful product of nature because it reflected variations in trait expressions. Influenced by evolutionary theory, Galton (1869) emphasized that natural selection requires variation amongst traits and interpreted variations observed amongst human phenomena (at the population level) as an indicator of human evolution and progression.

Fisher (1925), in articulating the procedures of ANOVA, contrasted the goals of modern statistics with those of earlier statisticians, explaining that it is a feature of modern statistics to be interested in studying variation rather than merely obtaining averages. Fisher (1925) further referenced and drew influence from Galton and his statistician colleague, Pearson, in examining co-variations amongst multiple variates using the methods of correlation. Although it may seem as if there is a lack of interpretation involved in the formulaic process of ANOVA used predominately today, Dr. Quantitative's adoption of the approach is based on interpretations of the mean and variation that trace their histories to scholars such as Galton and Fisher. These interpretations are based on beliefs about the nature of trait expression and human variation that shaped early scholars' ideas about how these concepts ought to be studied and interpreted.

Now, returning to the question of "significance," Dr. Quantitative employs Fisher's ANOVA in conjunction with NHST, an approach to inference in which an a priori null hypothesis is stated and a test statistic is compared with conditions outlined under the a priori null hypothesis being true. As discussed at the beginning of this chapter, researchers claim "significance" of their findings, meaning that they employ a decision to reject the null hypothesis, if the probability of their observed test statistic is smaller than a pre-set criterion (alpha), conditional on the null hypothesis being true. As mentioned at the beginning of this chapter, there has been a great deal of discussion and debate in statistical literature around *mis*interpretations of significance under NHST (see Gigerenzer, 2004; Grice, this volume; Slaney, this volume). Namely, NHST does not provide the probability of the null hypothesis being true, nor does statistical significance claimed under NHST indicate practical significance. In other words, it will not tell Dr. Quantitative whether her results are relevant or meaningful in a practical context. To circumvent this issue, it has become common practice to expect researchers to not only report significance levels, but to also report effect sizes that quantify the degree of departure between the observed test statistic (in this case, the mean BDI score), and its value under the null hypothesis (see Cohen, 1994; Grice, this volume). However, reporting effect sizes in itself does not solve the problem of interpretation at the heart of NHST misuse. Once an effect size is reported, the researcher must still *interpret* that effect to determine whether it is meaningful. To this end, it is common for psychological researchers to rely on pre-specified cut-offs of standardized effect sizes; however, even authors of these cut-offs acknowledge that they should not be used to replace a researcher's judgement (Cohen, 1994).

Indeed, Dr. Quantitative may, on the basis of carrying out an inferential test using the logic of NHST, make the claim that a mean score of 23 on the BDI is "statistically significant." Upon transforming this mean score into a standardized effect size, she might further consult a set of guidelines for interpretation, concluding that she has obtained a "small," "medium," or "large" effect. However, Dr. Quantitative will once again be faced with the challenge of interpreting the *meaning* of this finding and telling a story based on her research results. To achieve this, Dr. Quantitative must reflect on her shared cultural and linguistic understanding of concepts involved in the creation of the BDI, such as "depression" and "sadness." That is, Dr. Quantitative must return to the initial *qualitative* descriptions that were applied to the label values provided to test takers. Employing inferences about quantified *qualitative* descriptions of psychological phenomena will inherently always be an interpretative process.

The "quality" in quantitative research

There are several levels of interpretation at play in the activities of quantitative researchers. Beyond the technically constrained statistical interpretation of the mean, researchers must also engage with their data to determine *why* the mean is a *meaningful* statistic for their research purposes. What does the mean *represent?* For Quetelet, it was "l'homme moyen;" whereas, for Galton, it was deviations from the mean, rather than the mean itself, that were most salient for representing human variation and progress. Moreover, once these tools have been implemented, researchers must interpret the research story, which may involve the activity of theory-building. In doing so, they must connect their results to culture, language, history, and biology. This requires them to step outside of the highly technical language of statistics to the more dynamic and complex grammar of everyday discourse. Undoubtedly, just as Quetelet's and Galton's lived experiences, values, and beliefs influenced their interpretations of statistical concepts, the modern quantitative researcher will also use their own subjective experiences to interpret their analyses.

Given that quantitative methods are an inherently interpretative enterprise, is there a "qualitative" aspect to quantitative research? As mentioned previously, the domain of qualitative research is heavily influenced by hermeneutics, or the study of interpretation; as such, the concept of "interpretation" is often explicitly used as an analytic device in qualitative research pursuits. However, a hermeneutic perspective does not require that one always be explicit or even aware of their own interpretations in order for them be engaged in such interpretation. On the contrary, hermeneutic scholars have posited the idea that *all* human activity is inherently interpretative (Gadamer, 2013; Heidegger, 1927). Building walls around the qualitative research community based on the notion that these researchers are more engaged in interpretation and meaning-making than quantitative researchers ignores a core concept in hermeneutics: the *nature of being is interpretative* and, therefore, human sciences as a human activity will *always* be interpretative, regardless of methodological approach (Gadamer, 2013; Heidegger, 1927).

Dr. Quantitative is not so different from her colleague, Dr. Qualitative. Both speak the same common language, share similar cultural values, and possibly even reside in the same community. They will each bring these shared cultural characteristics to their research activities; however, they will also bring their individual lived experiences. As such, there will be differences in their approaches to research. Dr. Quantitative was trained to attempt to withhold interpretation, minimize bias, and to view research as a much more rigid procedure than Dr. Qualitative. In turn, Dr. Qualitative was trained in hermeneutics and is openly aware of his own biases and interpretations. He further explicitly incorporates his interpretations as part of his analytical process. It appears then, that what separates these researchers is not whether they each engage in an interpretative research activity, but rather whether they are *aware of* and *acknowledge* that interpretative process, or if they actively attempt to *deny* it.

The lack of awareness and, sometimes, outright denial of the interpretative nature of quantitative methods has the potential to be detrimental to research in psychology in at least two critical ways. First, denial of the subjective aspects of quantitative methods creates a divide between quantitative and qualitative methods. Qualitative research becomes shunned from the psychological research community for fear that it introduces subjectivity into what is incorrectly believed to be a research process void of interpretation. Second, being unaware of their own interpretative biases, quantitative researchers are particularly susceptible to what Teo (2010) has termed, "epistemological violence."

Throughout the history of quantification in psychology, it is readily apparent that marginalized groups of people, including women and ethnic minorities, have been "othered" on the basis of the results of psychological research. Quantitative researchers drawing conclusions and presenting those conclusions as factual knowledge without regard for the interpretative process from which they were produced has led to such groups being described as inferior to privileged members of Western society. Lack of reflection on one's interpretative processes creates a pathway to ideologies that have the potential to disadvantage groups of individuals who are conceptualized as being inferior within that ideology (Gadamer, 2013). Examples of this are abound in the history of psychology and statistics, most notably, within the Eugenics and Craniometry movements of the late 19th and early 20th centuries, but also more recently within the enterprise of intelligence testing (Gould, 1981).

Welcoming interpretation into quantitative research

Although quantitative methods have always been fundamentally based on human values (see Zyphur & Pierides, 2019), psychological researchers today often neglect the interpretative nature of their methodological tools. Rather, it is presumed that knowledge in the field of psychology is attained through the mechanical implementation of methodological procedures. Quantitative researchers cling to their methodological rules as if such rules will undoubtedly lead them to the discovery of truth, void of any interpretative influence (Davidson, 2018). Such blind methodolatry (worship of quantitative methods; see Bakan, 1967; Slaney, this volume) closes the doors to research practices that openly acknowledge the interpretative nature of human activity, namely, qualitative research. However, methodolatry can be combatted through education. As an instructor, I have the option to delve deeper when my students ask questions regarding the natures of statistical concepts. I can incorporate the role of interpretation into the quantitative research process, illuminating quantitative methodological approaches as subjective human activities rather than presenting them as mechanical tools impervious to interpretation. This recommendation is not a new one. Quantitative methodologists have argued for the incorporation of culture into the statistics classroom while also urging psychologists who adopt NHST to not only present but to also interpret effect sizes in their research reports (see Davidson, 2018; Nolan & Simon, 2018). At the same time, qualitative researchers must also give credit to the interpretative nature of quantitative methods. *All* researchers are part of an interpretative community that strives to make meaning from research data, whether that data be represented numerically, textually, or visually. Acknowledging the interpretative nature of all human research activity will not only open the door to qualitative methods in psychology, but also enrich the use of quantitative methods in the field.

References

American Psychological Association. (2012). *APA guidelines for the undergraduate Psychology major* (Version 2.0). www.apa.org/ed/precollege/about/psymajor-guidelines.pdf.

Bakan, D. (1967). *On method: Toward a reconstruction of psychological investigation*. San Francisco: Jossey-Bass.

Beck, A.T., Ward, C. H., Mendelson, M., Mock, J., & Erbaugh, J. (1961) An inventory for measuring depression. *Archives of General Psychiatry*, 4, 561–571.

Brinkmann, S., Jacobsen, M. H., & Kristiansen, S. (2014). Historical overview of qualitative research in the social sciences. In P. Leavy (Ed.), *The Oxford handbook of qualitative research* (pp. 17–42). Oxford: Oxford University Press.

Cohen, J. (1994). The Earth is round (p < .05). *American Psychologist*, 49, 997–1003.

Davidson, I. (2018). The ouroboros of psychological methodology: The case of effect sizes (mechanical objectivity vs. expertise). *Review of General Psychology*, *22*(4), 469–476.

Denzin, N. K. & Lincoln, Y. S. (2005a). Introduction: The discipline and practice of qualitative research. In N. K. Denzin & Y. S. Lincoln (Eds.), *The sage handbook of qualitative research* (3rd ed.) (pp. 1–32). Thousand Oaks, CA: Sage.

Denzin, N. K. & Lincoln, Y. S. (2005b). Preface. In N. K. Denzin & Y. S. Lincoln (Eds.), *The sage handbook of qualitative research* (3rd ed.) (pp. ix–xix). Thousand Oaks, CA: Sage.

Fisher, R. A. (1925). *Statistical methods for research workers*. Edinburgh: Oliver and Boyd.

Fisher, R. A. (1935). *The design of experiments* (5th ed.). Edinburgh: Oliver and Boyd.

Fisher, R. A. (1956). *Statistical methods and scientific inference*. Edinburgh: Oliver and Boyd.

Gadamer, H. (2013). *Truth and method* (J. Weinsheimer & D. G. Marshall, Revised Trans.). London: Bloomsbury. (Original work published 1975).

Galton, F. (1869). *Hereditary genius*. London: Macmillan.

Gigerenzer, G. (2004). Mindless statistics. *Journal of Socio-Economics*, *33*, 587–606.

Glaser, B. G. & Strauss, A. L. (1967). *The discovery of grounded theory: Strategies for qualitative research*. New Brunswick, NJ: Aldine Transaction.

Gould, S. J. (1981). *The mismeasure of man*. New York: Norton.

Gravetter, F. J. & Wallnau, L. B. (2013). *Statistics for the behavioral sciences.* Boston, MA: Wadsworth.

Heidegger, M. (1927). *Sein und zeit.* De Gruyter. English translation by J. Stambaugh (1996), *Being and time.* New York: State University of New York Press.

Howell, D. C. (2010). *Statistical methods for psychology* (7th ed.). Belmont, CA: Wadsworth.

Husserl, E. (2008). *Logical investigations* (Vol. 1) (J. N. Findlay, Trans.). Milton Park: Routledge. (Original work published 1900/1901).

James, W. (1907). *Pragmatism: A new name for some old ways of thinking.* Cambridge, MA: Harvard University Press.

Lamiell, J. T. (2003). *Beyond individual and group differences: Human individuality, scientific psychology, and William Stern's critical personalism.* Thousand Oaks, CA: Sage.

Lamiell, J. T. (2019). Some historical perspectives on the marginalization of qualitative methods within mainstream scientific psychology. In B. Schiff (Ed.). *Situating qualitative methods in psychological science* (pp. 11–26). New York: Routledge.

Lehmann, E. L. (1993). The Fisher, Neyman-Pearson theories of testing hypotheses: One theory or two? *Journal of the American Statistical Association,* 88(424), 1242–1249.

Michell, J. (2004). *Measurement in psychology: A critical history of a methodological concept.* Cambridge: Cambridge University Press.

Neyman, J. & Pearson, E. S. (1933). On the problem of the most efficient tests of statistical hypotheses. *Philosophical Transactions of the Royal Society of London,* 231, 289–337.

Nolan, S. A. & Simon, S. F. (2018). Why culture matters in teaching statistics. In K. Keith (Ed.). *Culture across the curriculum: A psychology teacher's handbook.* Cambridge: Cambridge University Press.

Patton, M. Q. (2002). *Qualitative research and evaluation methods.* Thousand Oaks, CA: Sage.

Porter, T. M. (1986). *The rise of statistical thinking: 1820–1900.* Princeton: Princeton University Press.

Quetelet, A. (1842). *A treatise on man and the development of his faculties.* Edinburgh: Chambers. (Original work published 1835).

Smith, J. A., Flowers, P., & Larkin, M. (2009). *Interpretative phenomenological analysis: Theory method and research.* London: Sage.

Stevens, S. S. (1946). On the theory of scales of measurement. *Science,* 103, 677–680.

Stevens, S. S. (1958). Measurement and man. *Science,* 127, 383–389.

Teo, T. (2010). What is epistemological violence in the empirical sciences? *Social and Personality Psychology Compass,* 4/5, 295–303.

Tukey, J. W. (1977). *Exploratory Data Analysis.* Reading, MA: Addison-Wesley.

Wertz, F. J., Charmaz, K., McMullen, L M., Josselson, R., Anderson, R., & McSpadden, E. (2011). *Five ways of doing qualitative analysis: Phenomenological psychology, grounded theory, discourse analysis, narrative research, and intuitive inquiry*. New York: Guildford Press.

Willig, C. (2017). Interpretation in qualitative research. In C. Willig & W. S. Rogers (Eds.). *The sage handbook of qualitative research in psychology* (pp. 276–290) (2nd ed.). Thousand Oaks, CA: Sage.

Zyphur, M. J. & Pierides, D. C. (2019). Statistics and probability have always been value-laden: An historical ontology of quantitative research methods. *Journal of Business Ethics*. https://doi.org/10.1007/s10551-019-04187-8.

7 Is there a waning appetite for critical methodology in psychology?

Kathleen L. Slaney

The discipline of psychology is no stranger to crisis. However, psychology has also been no stranger to critique, from both within and beyond its disciplinary boundaries. Critical debates have concerned everything from its theoretical and philosophical foundations and scientific status to general and particular critiques of the methods and methodology which have been sanctioned and privileged within in. Thus, it would appear there has been at least some amount of critical scrutiny of the methodological approaches and practices of psychology *by* psychologists. In fact, recent discourse surrounding replication, the publication of fraudulent research findings, and the legitimacy of null hypothesis statistical testing (NHST[1]) have raised the specter of whether psychological science may have reached the level of full-blown crisis and the possibility that much of what psychological researchers do in the course of conducting research and disseminating research findings needs to be seriously rethought.

Yet, it appears that the key messages coming out of such critical methodological debates within psychology have not reached the researchers who use methods and attempt to advance or apply theory on the basis of the findings that result from their use. Whether due to lack of awareness, apathy, or resistance to enacting methodological change, one sees very little evidence of critical engagement with methodological theory and practice among psychological researchers. Although it might be understandable (if perhaps ultimately self-defeating) that advocates of mainstream approaches and methods would be resistant to more drastic critiques of disciplinary practices—i.e., those that endorse an abandonment of the entire enterprise—it is perplexing that critiques that retain a general commitment to the forms of empirical inquiry and methods upon which contemporary psychological science is founded have gained so little traction.

The discrepancy between critical methodologists' and empirical researchers' respective acknowledgements and attempts to remedy psychology's methodological problems complicates how one might approach the examination of the topic that is the focus of the present volume: scientific psychology's problematic research practices and general inertia, or incorrigibility, when it comes to methodological change and renewal in response to critique. On the one hand, psychological science could be characterized as both reasonably open to and capable of methodological change, as there's no denying that there have been over the history of the discipline alterations to methodological conventions and uses of specific methods in response to critique. On the other hand, there is no denying that persistent critique of certain methods has had minimal measurable impact on psychological researchers' uses of them and interpretations made on the basis of them. The enduring perseverance of NHST (Cumming et al., 2007; Oakes, 1986) and the conflating of aggregate with both general and individual level inferences (Bakan, 1966; Lamiell, 2015, this volume) are two clear examples of psychology's tenacious methodological incorrigibility. How does one reconcile these inconsistencies regarding psychologists' (lack of) appetite for internal methodological critique and, ultimately, methodological change? It is this question the proposed chapter aims to address.

The chapter begins with a brief survey of the history of crisis and critique in psychology, with an emphasis on critical methodology, highlighting a number of major methodological critiques that have appeared in mainstream psychological discourse. The general question of whether psychological science truly suffers from a persistent resistance to methodological critique and, if so, to what extent is then examined. This involves exploring both where and in what ways psychological science is and is not methodologically inert, or incorrigible. To that end, I explore the distinctions between different types of methodological critique, and both the extent to which each might be considered *restitutive* or *radical* and whether they have had a clear impact on research practice.

Crisis in psychology

The historical literature suggests that psychology has, in one sense or another, always been in crisis (Morawski, 2019; Teo, 2005). Psychology had barely settled into its status as an independent discipline in Europe and North America when Willy (1899) published *Die Krisis in der Psychologie* [The Crisis in Psychology], in which he claimed that the discipline was suffering from a chronic crisis (Teo, 2005). In 1925, German biologist and philosopher Hans Driesch published a booklet, also titled *The Crisis of Psychology*, asserting the need for psychology to decide upon a clear focus and direction (Allesch, 2012). In his 2005 book, *The Critique of Psychology*, Teo documented the history of both internal and external critique of psychology. Two important implications for the current discussion of his work are that the history of critical psychology is long (in fact, predating the formalization of psychology as an independent discipline) and that such critique has often been accompanied by a "vision for a better psychology and the promise to solve the theoretical, methodological, and practical problems of the discipline" (p. vii). Goertzen (2008) also tracked the history of crisis within psychology, highlighting that the crisis literature in psychology has been "substantially intertwined" with discussions of psychology's status as a science (e.g., Koch, 1981) but also notes a lack of consensus among crisis criers regarding the meaning of the term 'crisis' (see also Morawski, 2019). As such, the crisis literature is itself fragmented and, tends to perpetuate rather than provide a unified resolution for psychology's long-standing crisis.

Crises of a more explicitly methodological nature also have a long history within psychology. NHST has been shrouded in at least some amount of crisis for its entire history, with the debate surrounding its utility for psychological research heating up considerably over the last few decades. More recently, crisis in psychology has implicated the lack of replicability of research findings, highly publicized instances of fraud, and the prevalence of an array of practices falling under the umbrella banner of *questionable research practices* (QRPs; John, Loewenstein & Prelec, 2012; see also Pashler & Wagenmakers, 2012; Open Science Collaboration, 2015).

I shall examine more closely the critical works of some of the more well-celebrated critics within psychology in the next section. For the time being, suffice it to say that crisis has been with us for a very long time, and it has often been directed at methods and methodology. One might view such "critical methodology"[2] as a subdomain of scholarship within the discipline, although not all who have engaged in scholarship of this sort have explicitly characterized it as such. More often, these "critical methodologists" have been well-established psychological theorists and researchers who have witnessed and then publicly expressed their concerns about problems with theory and method in the discipline.

A history of critical methodology within psychology

As noted, methodological debates within psychology have been public enough to enter into the mainstream discourse of psychology and, in some cases, have left their footprint on how we use and teach certain methods today. Although there is a great deal of variety in terms of both the substance and approach adopted by critically minded commentators on theoretical and practical issues related to psychological methods, for the present purposes I have categorized them into three broad areas referenced, perhaps crudely, by the following labels: (1) *Some things are broke but just need a tune-up*; (2) *Many things are broke and an overhaul is needed*; (3) *It's a write-off and should be scrapped*. Brief descriptions and examples of each are provided.

Some things are broke but just need a tune-up

This first category includes psychological methodologists and researchers who acknowledge psychological methods are not perfect and some corrections and adjustments may be needed in order to maximize their utility for conducting rigorous and productive empirical research. Generally speaking, methodological critics within this camp do not call into question either the ontologically objectivist-realist and epistemically positivist-naturalist frameworks that dominate within the discipline. Nor do they tend to question whether the hegemonic methodological frame-work used in psychological research (i.e., use of quantitative measures, experimentation, and statistical analysis) is the right one. Rather, critiques of this type concern misuses, misapplications, or misunderstandings of conventional psychological methods. This category makes up the largest of critically minded methodologists and researchers in psychology.

It is difficult to choose a single or even a handful of particularly striking examples of this type of methodological critique given how pervasive it is and, also, because it is a necessary part of the common-place activity of any empirical science. Issuing correctives regarding conventional methods and interpretations made on the basis of them is just something scientists do. As such, there is a long and vast literature from which to draw examples but many of these are fairly mundane and, therefore, not very interesting. However, there is a relatively recent body of empirical research on journal reporting practices, which I will summarize briefly, that exemplifies well this category of critical meth-odology. This literature falls into one of three rough areas: (1) general reporting standards for studies involving conventional experimental or correlative designs and quantitative data collection and analysis; and specific reporting standards for (2) meta-analysis and (3) psycho-metric evaluations. Space constraints prohibit me elaborating on spe-cific works. However, the unified message in critical methodology of this type is that psychological researchers are either unaware of or are flouting methodological "rules" or misinterpreting empirical findings generated from specific methods (most notably the methods associated with NHST). The general objective of critical methodologists in this category, thus, is to sound the alarm and alert psychological researchers to discipline-wide standards with the hope that this will suffice to correct the problem. In addition, specific task forces (e.g., the Task Force on Statistical Inference [TFSI]) and working groups (e.g., APA Working Group on Journal Article Reporting Standards [JARS]) have been formed and produced explicit guidelines to aid researchers (e.g., APA, 2008; Appelbaum et al., 2018; Wilkinson & the TFSI, 1999). This has, in turn, resulted in a body of critical methodology aimed at tracking whether these and other correctives are working.

Many things are broke and an overhaul is needed

The second category includes methodologists and researchers who are far more concerned than those in the previous category about the extent of methodological problems, and much less hopeful that there exist solutions that would not require major reforms to methodological theory and research practice. These critical methodologists and researchers examine more deeply the theoretical and philosophical foundations of commonly employed methods and appeal for, at least, a broadening psychological methodology to include alternative methods and, sometimes, alternative epistemic frameworks.

There are many well-known methodological critics from this camp who have commented on a vast array of methodological topics, including psychological measurement (e.g., Krantz, 1968; Luce & Tukey, 1964; Michell, 1999), validation of psychological tests and assessment procedures (e.g., Campbell & Fiske, 1959; Cronbach & Meehl, 1955; Messick, 1988), experimental validity (e.g., Campbell & Stanley, 1963), the many limitations of NHST hegemony and practice (e.g., Bakan, 1966; Cumming, 2014; Cohen, 1994; Gigerenzer, 1998; Lykken, 1968; Oakes, 1986; Rozeboom, 1960), and, more recently, replication (e.g., Pashler & Wagenmakers, 2012; Open Science Collaboration, 2015), research fraud and other forms of corruption (e.g., Chambers, 2017), researcher "degrees of freedom" (Simmons, Nelson, & Simonsohn, 2011) and other QRPs (e.g., John, Loewenstein, & Prelec, 2012).

However, arguably no one represents a greater volume and breath of contribution to critical methodology in psychology than Paul Meehl. He was trained as both a clinical and research psychologist, but his interests varied broadly, and he penetrated deeply the theoretical, philosophical, and practical dimensions of both the science and practice of psychology. Over the course of his five-decade career, Meehl penned over 180 books, book chapters, and journal articles, weighing in on a vast array of topics, including: theoretical versus empirical constructs (MacCorquodale & Meehl, 1948); validity and validation of psychological tests and measures (Cronbach & Meehl, 1955); measurement and theory of personality (Meehl & Hathaway, 1946); clinical assessment versus actuarial prediction (Meehl, 1954); schizophrenia (Meehl, 1962); taxometric modeling (Meehl 1992); and a range of philosophy of science topics. Meehl had a deeply discerning eye for the complex philosophical dimensions of scientific psychology and was an avid and active promoter of critical progressive development of scientific psychology. In a highly-cited article published in 1978, Meehl listed 20 "intrinsic subject matter difficulties" related to the lack of cumulative character of knowledge in the "soft" areas of psychology (in which he included clinical, counseling, social, personality, community, and school psychology) that "make human psychology hard to scientize" (Meehl, 1978, pp. 806–807). He implicated NHST in particular, boldly asserting that "the almost universal reliance on merely refuting the null hypothesis as the standard method for corroborating substantive theories in the soft areas is a terrible mistake, is basically unsound, poor scientific strategy, and one of the worst things that ever happened in the history of psychology" (p. 817), adding "that the whole business is so radically defective as to be scientifically almost pointless" (p. 823).[3]

But given his clear disdain for what was then and continues today to be the most widely used general method within psychology, why choose Meehl an exemplar of critical methodologists in this second category? Two primary reasons. First, because despite his sophisticated diagnoses and prognoses of the theoretical and methodological problems of psychology, Meehl remained throughout his career a staunch advocate for a science of psychology based on an objectivist-realist philosophy and the rigorous application of quantitative assessment and experimental and statistical methods (Slaney, 2017). To be sure, his was a clarion call for psychology to substantially clean up its act, including by rejecting outmoded methods and philosophies of science and endorsing what he (and others) argued were more fitting ones. But he was not by any means advocating the abandonment of the notion that psychology belongs among the ranks of other sciences and can be—with a sustained focus on substantially improving both theory and method— a most productive and generative scientific discipline. Second, Meehl's legacy of critical methodology had and continues to have ripple effects in the works of his former students and close colleagues, as well as for the many who have been inspired by, modeled their work after, or otherwise endorsed (or critiqued) one or more areas of his scholarship (e.g.,

Cicchetti & Grove, 1991; Waller et al., 2006). Moreover, it is in the spirit of the great Paul Meehl that many current critical methodologists continue to sound the call for scientific reform in psychology.

It's a write-off and should be scrapped

A third category—and smallest of the three—encompasses critical scholars who question at root the importation of the methods and methodologies of the natural sciences into psychology. Relatively few of the individuals who could be categorized in this group are methodologists or writing specifically about methodological issues, but many have substantial historical and philosophical training or acumen.[4] Many reject, or at least seriously question, whether psychology should be considered an extension of the natural sciences, or a science at all. Some diagnose psychology as suffering from the intractable problem of "methodolatry" (Bakan, 1961, as cited in Teo, 2005), that is, of conceptualizing its subject matter through its methods and methodology as opposed to choosing methods that are appropriately suited to the subject matter that defines the psychological domain (Teo, 2005).

Sigmund Koch is a prominent figure whose critical work falls well within this category. Although a strong advocate of behaviorism early in his career, Koch dramatically changed his perspective in mid-career, after which he spent the remainder of his career arguing that "psychology is not a single or coherent discipline but rather a collectivity of studies of varied cast, some few of which may qualify as science, while most do not" (Koch, 1981, p. 268). Psychology's self-declared "anti-hero" (Koch, 1977), Koch argued that it made better sense to conceive of psychology not as a cohesive discipline but rather as a set of "psychological studies." If the latter are to yield any genuine knowledge of "psychological events," … "problems must be approached with humility, methods must be contextual and flexible, and anticipations of synoptic breakthrough must be held in check" (Koch, 1981, p. 268).

Kurt Danziger and Jan Smedslund are also two critical scholars that arguably could also be said to fall within this third category. In his 1990 book, *Constructing the Subject*, Danziger traced the history of psychological research methodology, providing a compelling account of the socially constructed nature of the methods, subjects, and knowledge of psychological science. Smedslund developed "psychologic" (PL), a system of axioms, definitions, corollaries and theorems, and used these to demonstrate that mainstream scientific psychology is "pseudoempirical," that is, appears to be concerned with testing scientific hypotheses that are empirical and contingent but what can be shown in most cases to be a priori and noncontingent (Smedslund, 1988). He further contended, thus, a psychology based in experimentation and statistical methods could not bear the fruit of revealing psychological laws as has been desired by psychological researchers throughout much of the history of the discipline.

It is important to recognize that the three categories I have presented here are loose and by no means presumed to be exhaustive of the many nuanced perspectives and positions psychological researchers hold with respect to the methods used and defended by some members of the discipline and scrutinized and rejected by others. It also bears mentioning that some critics could be categorized into more than one category due either to offering critiques of different types on different topics or shifting the nature of their critiques over time.[5] If one accepts that critical methodologists vary in ways similar to how I have characterized, what does this imply for whether their critical messages get taken up by psychological researchers?

Is the appetite really waning? Two important considerations

Clearly, the sheer amount of recent commentary on psychology's replication and other crises indicates the appetite for critical methodology continues, at least in some quarters. However, the question of which quarters and with which intended consequences remains somewhat muddied. I believe that some clarity can be offered by contemplating two important considerations that bear on the question of whether the appetite for methodological criticism in psychology is waning. The first concerns implications of the different types of methodological critique, the second an apparent disjunction between respective perspectives of methodologists and researchers regarding whether, and if so where, methodological problems persist.

Restitutive versus radical methodological critique

It cannot be disputed that psychology has a long and active history of critique. Though, it is less clear the extent to which critical methodologists in psychology have been generally aligned in terms of both the nature of their critiques and implied consequences these may have for practice or, ultimately, for the status of the discipline. In the immediately preceding section, I identified three rough categories of methodological critique. These, I believe can be sorted (again, roughly) into two superordinate categories which I will call *restitutive* and *radical*. Whereas the goal of restitutive critical methodology is primarily to issue correctives regarding current methodological practice, it does not challenge in a serious way the methodological foundations of mainstream psychological science. Of the three categories identified above, the first falls squarely within the restitutive class. For example, there have been many cogent critiques of NHST and the problems (e.g., file drawer problem) and QRPs that are associated with it (e.g., p-hacking; flawed interpretations of p-values; lack of Type II error control), wherein useful correctives are issued (e.g., reporting effect size and error estimates; differentiating clearly between statistical and practical significance) (see Nickerson, 2000). Such calls for change are unequivocal that reform is needed but generally do not imply an abandonment of NHST (see Harlow, Mulaik, & Steiger, 1997). More recent appeals to recognize the problems undergirding widespread failures to replicate psychological research findings and solutions that have been put forth (e.g., preregistration of studies, open data) are also primarily restitutive in spirit (e.g., Nosek & Bar-Anan, 2012; Nosek, Spies, & Motyl, 2012; Simmons, Nelson, & Simonsohn, 2011).

Radical critical methodology, conversely, involves much deeper examinations of the methodological foundations of psychological science and oftentimes promotes alternative frameworks and methods for psychological inquiry. The second and third categories described above could both be considered radical, however, the two differ by degree. Whereas critiques in the second category are radical in terms of calling for extensive methodological reform, they are ultimately restitutive in spirit in that the methodological reforms proposed are intended to improve the theoretical, methodological, and technical rigor of an ontologically objectivist-realist and epistemically positivist-naturalist scientific psychology, rather than deconstruct or replace it. However, those in the third category oftentimes call for a substantial or complete reworking of the epistemic frame and some call for a reconsideration of the status of psychology as a science. Appeals to replace NHST with the "new statistics" (e.g., Cumming 2014) or Bayesian frameworks (e.g., Kruschke & Liddell, 2018) are good examples of more moderately radical methodological critique, as they maintain a strong commitment to measurement, experimentation, and statistical analysis as a methodological foundation for scientific psychology. In contrast, critical scholarship that appeals to more essential reworkings of psychology's basic epistemic (e.g., Teo, 2017; Martin, this volume; see also Sugarman & Martin, 2020) and methodological frameworks (e.g., Grice, this volume; Yanchar, Gantt, & Clay, 2005; see also Martin, Sugarman, & Slaney, 2015) exemplify a more radically critical methodology.

A disconnect between methodologists and researchers

A consistent outcome from the empirical research on journal reporting practices summarized briefly above is that there has been and continues to be significant disconnection between methodologists and researchers. To put it simply: psychological researchers for the most part have missed the memo that Venice is sinking! For example, despite the long-standing and loud outcries over the problems and limitations of NHST, psychological researchers overwhelming continue to (mis) use hypothesis testing as a primary method (Cumming et al., 2007; Sharpe, 2013), albeit with some small improvements (e.g., increased reporting of effect sizes). Similar disconnections have been documented with respect to assessment and reporting of psychometric and validity information (e.g., Slaney, 2017) and meta-analysis (e.g., Hohn, Slaney, Tafreshi, 2020).

But why does this disconnect between psychological methodologists and psychological researchers exist? There are, no doubt, many reasons including researchers' lack of awareness of statistical developments; insufficient methodological training; challenges obtaining or operating statistical software; lack of oversight or enforcement by journals or professional organizations; pressures to publish; too few methodologists acting as "mavens" (Sharpe, 2013); as well as lack of access to the methods discourse and very little if any training in critical inquiry such that researchers can understand and make informed decisions about different methodological options (Slaney, 2015; Tafreshi, this volume; Yanchar et al., 2005). There is likely also a kind of mundane pragmatism at work: measurement, experimentation, and statistical analysis "work" in the sense that researchers always get a "finding" thereby seemingly obviating the need to mess with the status quo.

A clear implication of the disconnect between methodologists and researchers is that the solutions that have been put forward with the intention of improving psychological research practices have not had widespread impact. It is important to consider the distinction between restitutive and radical critiques here. For the most part, where improvements have been made these have been in response to the lowest hanging fruit of restitutive critiques (e.g., providing estimates of effect; emphasizing the distinction between statistical and practical "significance"). Not surprisingly, changes implied by radical critiques, even ones that are ultimately restitutive, have gained no appreciable traction when it comes to altering the research practices of most psychological researchers. It may be too soon to tell whether the recent proposals for reform will fare better but, given the radical nature of some of the proposed changes (e.g., mandatory preregistration and open data; Nosek, Ebersole, Dehaven, & Mellor, 2018), history does not bode well for the prospect.

Concluding remarks

According to Ioannidis (2012, p. 245), "The ability to self-correct is considered a hallmark of science" but "self-correction does not always happen ... by default." Indeed, the very fact of the current crises surrounding the lack of replicability of research findings and persistent prevalence of QRPs, both of which prominent methodologists have long recognized and warned about, is a strong testament to psychology's persistent inertia when it comes to learning from the lessons of our past.

A more direct answer to the question that forms the title of this chapter, "Is there a waning appetite for critical methodology in psychology?," is "yes" ... "no" ... "maybe?" In all seriousness, as the other chapters in this volume—and the body of work they collectively summarize—indicate, there is an abundance of evidence that fair and sound—and repeated—critiques of the dominate methodological tools of mainstream scientific psychology seem to be mostly falling on deaf ears, despite some small improvements in reporting and some growing movement towards greater transparency. Most of the latter I would diagnose as restitutive. Few have been dramatically reformative, and virtually none have been radical. In 1991, Lykken appealed to psychological researchers that we take a "frank look at ourselves" and make "an honest assessment of our symptoms and defects" (p. 4). It is arguable that until there exists appreciation within psychology for that kind of deep and careful critical and historical analysis of our methods and methodology, the appetite for critical methodology is likely to continue to be sated by small and relatively inconsequential adjustments to the dominant hegemony.

Notes

1 Nickerson (2000) notes the 'S' in NHST is used by some to refer to 'statistical' and to others to refer to 'significance.' Herein, 'NHST' will be used to denote either usage.
2 Note that Yanchar, Gantt, and Clay (2005) imply a different usage of this term than I intend here. Whereas theirs refers to an alternative approach to human science research founded on methodological pragmatism, I take the

term to refer broadly to scholarship which involves the critical examination of both general methodology and specific methods.

3 Attesting to the lack of pronounced effect of Meehl's lessons, in 1991 Lykken recapitulated and extended many of the themes in Meehl (1978) and, 20 years later, Woods (2011) examined Lykken's criticisms and conclusions, only to find that still very little progress had been made within psychology with respect to the issues raised by Meehl and, again, by Lykken.

4 Much of the scholarship of the contributors of the current volume, as well as that of many current or past members of groups such as the Society of Theoretical and Philosophical Psychology (Division 24 of the APA), the History and Philosophy section of the Canadian Psychological Association, and the International Society for Theoretical and Philosophical Psychology, represents this category of "methodological" critique.

5 Of course, I could have also included the "It ain't broke so don't need fixing" and "We know it's broke but there ain't anything we can do about it" perspectives. However, I believe both are probably quite rare. The latter is likely to be held by only the most cynical and defeated methodological critics, the former by those with a tremendous amount to be gained by keeping the status quo (i.e., those with great prestige whose vitae are built out of research which has relied heavily on flawed or unsuitable methods).

References

Allesch, C. G. (2012). Hans Driesch and the problems of "normal psychology". Rereading his Crisis in Psychology (1925). *Studies in the History and Philosophy of Biological and Biomedical Sciences, 43,* 455–461.

APA Publications and Communications Board Working Group on Journal Article Reporting Standards. (2008). Reporting standards for research in psychology: Why do we need them? What might they be? *American Psychologist, 63,* 839–851. doi: 10.1037/0003-066X.63.9.839.

Appelbaum, M., Cooper, H., Kline, R. B., Mayo-Wilson, E., Nezu, A. M., & Rao, S. M. (2018). Journal article reporting standards for quantitative research in psychology: The APA Publications and Communications Board task force report. *American Psychologist, 73*(1), 3–25. doi: 10.1037/amp0000191.

Bakan, D. (1966). The test of significance in psychological research. *Psychological Bulletin, 66,* 423–437.

Campbell, D. T. & Fiske, D. W. (1959). Convergent and discriminant validation by the multitrait-multimethod matrix. *Psychological Bulletin, 56,* 81–105.

Campbell, D. T., & Stanley, J. C. (1963). *Experimental and quasi-experimental designs for research.* Boston: Houghton Mifflin Company.

Chambers, C. (2017). *The seven deadly sins of psychology.* Princeton, NJ: Princeton University Press.

Cicchetti, D., & Grove, W. M. (Ed.). (1991). *Thinking clearly about psychology: Essays in honor of Paul E. Meehl, Vol. 1. Matters of public interest; Vol. 2. Personality and psychopathology.* Minneapolis: University of Minnesota Press.

Cohen, J. (1994). The earth is round (p < .05). *American Psychologists, 49,* 997–1003.

Cooper, H. (2018). *Reporting quantitative research in psychology: How to meet APA style journal article reporting standards.* Washington, DC: American Psychological Association.

Cronbach, L. J. & Meehl, P. E. (1955). Construct validity and psychological tests. *Psychological Bulletin,* 52, 281–302.

Cumming, G. (2014). The new statistics: Why and how. *Psychological Science, 25,* 7–29.

Cumming. G., Fidler, F., Leonard, M., Kalinowski, P., Christiansen, A., Kleinig, A., Lo, J., McMenamin, N., & Wilson, S. (2007). Statistical reform in psychology: Is anything changing? *Psychological Science, 18,* 230–232.

Danziger, K. (1990). *Constructing the subject: Historical origins of psychological research.* Cambridge: Cambridge University Press.

Driesch, H. (1925). *The crisis in psychology.* Princeton, NJ: Princeton University Press.

Gigerenzer, G. (1998). We need statistical thinking, not statistical rituals. *Behavioral and Brain Sciences, 21,* 199–200.

Goertzen, J. R. (2008). On the possibility of unification: The reality and nature of the crisis in psychology. *Theory & Psychology, 18,* 829–852.

Harlow, L., Mulaik, S., & Steiger, J. (Eds.). (1997). *What if There Were no Significance Tests?* Hillsdale, NJ: Lawrence Erlbaum Associates.

Hohn, R., Slaney, K. L., & Tafreshi, D. (2020). An empirical review of meta-analytic research and reporting practices in psychology. *Review of General Psychology.* Advance online publication: doi:10.1177/1089268020918844.

Ioannidis, J. P. A. (2012). Why science is not necessarily self-correcting. *Psychological Science, 7,* 645–654.

John, L., Loewenstein, G., & Prelec, D. (2012). Measuring the prevalence of questionable research practices with incentives for truth telling. *Psychological Science, 23*(5), 524–532.

Koch, S. (1977, August). *Vagrant Confessions of an Asystematic Psychologist: An Intellectual Autobiography.* Invited address at the Annual Convention of the American Psychological Association, San Francisco, California.

Koch, S. (1981). The nature and limits of psychological knowledge: Lessons of a century qua "science." *American Psychologist, 36,* 257–269.

Krantz, D. H. (1968). A survey of measurement theory. In G. B. Dantzig & A. F. Veinott (Eds.), *Mathematics of the decision sciences, part 2* (pp. 314–350). New York: McGraw-Hill.

Kruschke, J. K., & Liddell, T. M. (2018). The Bayesian new statistics: Hypothesis testing, estimation, meta-analysis, and power analysis from a Bayesian perspective. *Psychonomic Bulletin & Review, 25,* 178–206.

Lamiell, J. T. (2015). Statistical thinking in psychological research: In quest of clarity through historical inquiry and conceptual analysis. In J. Martin, J. Sugarman, & K. L. Slaney (Eds.), *The Wiley handbook of theoretical and philosophical psychology: Methods, approaches, and new directions for social sciences* (pp. 200–215). Chichester: Wiley Blackwell.

Lamiell, J. T. (this volume). On the persistent systemic misuse of statistical methods within mainstream psychology. In J. T. Lamiell & K. L. Slaney (Eds.), *Scientific psychology's problematic research practices and inertia: History, sources, and recommended solutions* (pp. 8–22). Routledge.

Luce, R. D., & Tukey, J. W. (1964). Simultaneous conjoint measurement: A new type of fundamental measurement. *Journal of Mathematical Psychology, 1,* 1–27.

Lykken, D. T. (1968). Statistical significance in psychological research. *Psychological Bulletin, 70,* 151–159.

Lykken, D. (1991). What's wrong with psychology anyway? In D. Cichetti & W. Grove (Eds.), *Thinking clearly about psychology: Essays in honor of Paul E. Meehl, Vol. 1: Matters of public interest* (pp. 3–39). Minneapolis, MN: University of Minnesota Press.

MacCorquodale, K., & Meehl, P. E. (1948). On a distinction between hypothetical constructs and intervening variables. *Psychological Review, 55,* 95–107.

Messick, S. (1980). Test Validity and the ethics of assessment. *American Psychologist, 35,* 1021–1027.

Martin, J. (this volume). Psychology's struggle with understanding persons. In J. T. Lamiell & K. L. Slaney (Eds.), *Scientific psychology's problematic research practices and inertia: History, sources, and recommended solutions* (pp. 102–115). Routledge.

Martin, J., Sugarman, J., & Slaney, K. L. (Eds.). (2015). The Wiley handbook of theoretical and philosophical psychology: Methods, approaches, and new directions for social sciences. Chichester: Wiley Blackwell.

Meehl, P. E. (1954). *Clinical versus statistical prediction: A theoretical analysis and a review of the evidence.* Minneapolis: University of Minnesota Press.

Meehl, P. E. (1962). Schizotaxia, schizotypy, schizophrenia. *American Psychologist, 17,* 827–838.

Meehl, P. (1978). Theoretical risks and tabular asterisks: Sir Karl, Sir Ronald, and the slow progress of soft psychology. *Journal of Consulting and Clinical Psychology, 46,* 806–834.

Meehl, P. E. (1992) Factors and taxa, traits and types, differences of degree and differences in kind. *Journal of Personality, 60,* 117–174.

Meehl, P. E. & Hathaway, S. R. (1946). The K factor as a suppressor variable in the Minnesota Multiphasic Personality Inventory. *Journal of Applied Psychology, 30,* 525–564.

Messick, S. (1988). The once and future issues of validity: Assessing the meaning and consequences of measurement. In H. Wainer & H.I. Braun (Eds.), *Test Validity.* (pp. 33–46). Hillsdale, NY: Lawrence Erlbaum Associates.

Michell, J. (1999). *Measurement in psychology: A critical history of a methodological concept.* Cambridge: Cambridge University Press.

Morawski, J. (2019). The replication crisis: How might philosophy and theory of psychology be of use? *Journal of Theoretical and Philosophical Psychology, 39,* 218–238.

Nickerson, R. S. (2000). Null hypothesis significance testing: A review of old and continuing controversy. *Psychological Methods, 2,* 241–301.

Nosek, B., & Bar-Anan, Y. (2012). Scientific utopia: I. Opening scientific communication. *Psychological Inquiry, 23,* 217–243.

Nosek, B., Ebersole, C., Dehaven, A., & Mellor, D. (2018). The preregistration revolution. *Proceedings of the National Academy of Sciences, 115*(11), 2600–2606.

Nosek, B. A., Spies, J. R., & Motyl, M. (2012). Scientific utopia: II. Restructuring incentives and practices to promote truth Over publishability. *Perspectives on Psychological Science, 7,* 615–631.

Oakes, M. (1986). *Statistical inference: A commentary for the social and behavioural sciences.* Chichester: John Wiley & Sons.

Open Science Collaboration (2015). Estimating the reproducibility of psychological science. *Science, 349,* doi: 10.1126/science.aac4716

Pashler, H., & Wagenmakers, E-J. (2012). Editors' introduction to the special section on replicability in psychological science: A crisis of confidence? *Perspectives on Psychological Science, 7,* 528–530.

Rozeboom, W. W. (1960). Studies in the empiricist theory of scientific meaning. *Philosophy of Science, 27,* 359–373.

Sharpe, D. (2013). Why the resistance to statistical innovations? Bridging the communication gap. *Psychological Methods, 18,* 572–582.

Simmons, J., Nelson, L., & Simonsohn, U. (2011). False-positive psychology. *Psychological Science, 22*(11), 1359–1366.

Slaney, K. L. (2015). "I'm Not That Kind of Psychologist": A Case for Methodological Pragmatism in Theoretical Inquiries into Psychological Science Practices. In J. Martin, J. Sugarman, & K. L Slaney (Eds.), *The Wiley handbook of theoretical and philosophical psychology: Methods, approaches, and new directions for social sciences* (pp. 343–358). Chichester: Wiley Blackwell.

Slaney, K. L. (2017). *Validating psychological constructs: Historical, philosophical, and practical dimensions.* Basingstoke: Palgrave Macmillan.

Smedslund, J. (1988). *Psycho-logic.* New York: Springer Verlag.

Sugarman, J., & Martin, J. (Eds.). (2020). *A psychological humanities of personhood.* New York: Routledge.

Tafreshi, D. (this volume). On the Interpretative Nature of Quantitative Methods and Psychology's Resistance to Qualitative Methods. In J. T. Lamiell & K. L. Slaney (Eds.), *Scientific psychology's problematic research practices and inertia: History, sources, and recommended solutions* (pp. 70–85). New York: Routledge.

Teo, T. (2005). *The critique of psychology: From Kant to postcolonial theory.* New York: Springer.

Teo, T. (2017). From psychological science to the psychological humanities: Building a general theory of subjectivity. *Review of General Psychology, 21,* 281–291.

Waller, N., Yonce, L., Grove, W., Faust, D., & Lenzenweger, M. (Eds.). (2006). *A Paul Meehl Reader.* New York: Routledge, https://doi.org/10.4324/9780203759554.

Wiggins, B. J., & Christopherson, C. D. (2019). The replication crisis in psychology: An overview for theoretical and philosophical psychology. *Journal of Theoretical and Philosophical Psychology, 49,* 202–217.

Wilkinson, L., & The APA Task Force on Statistical Inference. (1999). Statistical methods in psychology journals: Guidelines and explanations. *American Psychologist, 54,* 594–604. doi: 10.1037/0003-066X.54.8.594.

Willy, R. (1899). *Die Krisis in der Psychologie* [The crisis in psychology]. Leipzig: Reisland.

Woods, B. (2011). What's still wrong with psychology, anyway? Twenty slow years, three old issues, and one new methodology for improving psychological research. Unpublished Master's thesis.

Yanchar, S. C., Gantt, E. E., & Clay, S. L. (2005). On the nature of a critical methodology. *Theory & Psychology, 15,* 27–50.

8 Psychology's struggle with understanding persons

Jack Martin

The methods most frequently employed by psychologists are ill-suited for a psychology that aims to understand particular persons. Findings from the vast majority of psychological research are, at best, generalizations. They are not laws that reveal cause-effect relationships that govern the actions, understandings, and experiences of persons in ways that apply to all individuals or apply conditionally in ways that can be clearly specified. The sampling and statistical methods of most psychological research obscure rather than illuminate an understanding of individual persons and are incapable of predicting how any particular individual who participates in such studies might react to the psychological interventions or engage in the psychological processes being studied.

Persons are agents who defy lawful regularities in their psychological lives. Unlike physical objects in idealized laboratory settings, persons do not respond predictably to the myriad circumstances they encounter daily. As physical objects, we are governed by Newton's law of universal gravitation. As socio-culturally embedded psychological agents, we interpret ourselves within an interpersonal, societal, and situational surround that is not universal. Even within such niches, we are not necessarily bound by situational constraints and influences. Conventional psychological methodologies are not well attuned to the social, contextual, relational, and psychological lives of individual persons.

An appropriately comprehensive and contextualized inquiry into particular persons requires an in-depth, in situ, and interactive study of their lives over time and across situations. What is needed are biographical studies and writings that illuminate the specific contexts and conditions, interactivities and actions, experiences and purposes, achievements and losses that describe real persons' lives as actually lived. Fortunately, there exists a rich and varied history of biographical and life writing from which psychologists interested in the study of persons might draw.

The general and the particular

It is noteworthy that to date psychology has produced no scientific laws that apply to all persons and are accompanied by precise descriptions concerning the exact conditions under which they apply. Nothing remotely similar to Fourier's law of heat conduction has been discovered by psychologists. In all instances of the transmission of heat in materials, the heat flux is proportional to the negative gradient in the temperature and to the area, at right angles to that gradient, through which the heat flows. The statistical findings of psychologists do not hold true of all the relevant instances to which they possibly might apply. Indeed, so low and vague are the significance and reliability thresholds applied in statistical testing as employed in psychological research that it is not even possible to state with any degree of precision what the relevant conditions that attend such findings might be. To speak statistically is to speak of what is true on average in a way that is thought to be captured in quantitative representations. Something that holds true on average is not true of all the instances that contribute to the average and might not be true of any of those discrete instances. Although success in school may be highly correlated with measures of self-regulation, there are many successful students who score poorly on such measures and many low achievers who score highly on them (Vassallo, 2013). Indeed, it is even possible for a group in a group comparison study to be significantly superior to another group, based on common statistical tests, and yet for the majority of students in the superior group to display scores inferior to the average score for students in both groups (cf. Lamiell, 2003).

Findings from psychological research are not laws. At best, they are generalizations and unlike laws, generalizations admit to exceptions. Because it is not possible to specify the numerous influences on focal phenomena such as academic achievement and self-regulation, or most of the other phenomena that interest psychologists, predicting possible results of or exceptions to the findings of psychological research seldom is possible. So, what we are left with are generalizations that are not particularly general.

Data from psychological research never speak for themselves. Such data always must be interpreted by researchers and those who wish to apply the findings of research and claim an empirical basis for their applications. Strictly speaking, results of any scientific research must be interpreted. However, in the absence of lawful regularities and in consideration of the means by which psychological data are created through the theoretical and methodological practices of research psychologists, psychological data and their conditions of application require much greater levels of interpretation by those who attempt to use them (cf. Martin & Sugarman, 2009.

What then does the reasonable interpretation of psychological generalizations entail? It requires that users of the findings of psychological research must carefully consider the likelihood and the appropriateness with which generalizations from psychological research might apply to situations that interest them based on their knowledge and understanding of the particulars that define those situations. The difficulty of doing this is augmented by the facts that compared to researchers in the natural sciences, psychological researchers typically have much greater difficulty clearly conceptualizing the phenomena they are researching and much greater difficulty conducting strictly controlled experiments. What counts as academic achievement or self-regulation or other focal phenomena in psychological research and how to go about measuring them are highly contested. Such phenomena are difficult to capture adequately in controlled laboratory situations without changing them and how to capture and interpret them in complex classroom and other social contexts that include many other possible direct, mediating, and moderating influences is unclear.

The upshot is that general findings from psychological research always must be considered in relation to particulars—particular teachers, particular students, particular classrooms and schools, and so forth. Predicting the outcome of a specific instance of psychological research or applying results of psychological research in new contexts are always problematic. Despite any similarities that may exist, persons are unique individuals with diverse life histories who vary in attitudes, knowledge, interests, concerns, background, sociocultural and economic contexts, parenting, health, capabilities, and in a host of other personal and social ways.

The social and the personal

The fact that personhood is a dynamic, life-long achievement that develops in ways that are typically quite open-ended ensures that prescriptions based on psychological research are necessarily uncertain. As biological human beings, persons are born with phylogenetically selected predispositions to orient to the world and especially to other persons and to remember some of what we experience. These dispositions are present only in the most rudimentary forms at birth and continue to develop throughout individual lives in interaction with the world and others in it. In early infancy, children experience pre-reflectively. For example, after experiencing breast feeding or observing the movement of a crib mobile, the infant typically is able to re-orient to these objects. As growth and experience accumulate, the infant's abilities to orient and re-orient to the objects and world around itself increase dramatically. Cued and assisted by the bodily and facial movements of caregivers and others, young children follow the gazes of others and begin to use others' reactions as a basis for acting themselves. With frequent and increasing interaction in routine exchanges with others, children learn to coordinate their participation in simple practices that are repeated over and over again—for example, giving and receiving objects, touching and being touched, observing and performing simple actions, and playing games such as peek-a-boo and hide and seek. As Mead (1934) and many others have observed, such routine, coordinated social exchanges involve taking up related social positions such as hider and seeker. With such experiences of position exchange, the young child is able to recall and anticipate being in one position (e.g., seeker) while occupying the other position (e.g., hider). With the ability to recall and anticipate social interactions, children are able to coordinate in more complex ways with others, to sense and understand others' perspectives as similar to and different from their own, and to require less direct interactional experience to understand more of what is going on around them (Martin & Gillespie, 2010).

With the acquisition of language and the ability to imagine possibilities verbalized, even if not extant in more directly observable ways, the child experiences the social world inter-subjectively as well as interactively (Tomasello, 1999). As children are able to coordinate with others in both these ways, they learn to act toward and understand them as intentional agents, with perspectives and purposes that differ from their own. With age and greater social experience, direct and vicarious, the perspectives and possibilities which children can coordinate, imagine, and employ purposefully to guide their actions increase dramatically and become increasingly abstracted. Children become able to reflect, even to critique, their own points of view and opinions, to theorize about others and their life experiences, and to engage in social comparison and assessment. They are able to imagine how things might be different from what they are and react to these and other imaginings as well as to what actually is present and occurring around them. Eventually, a growing personal history of social interactivity and inter-subjectivity that enables increasingly sophisticated capabilities of imagination and interpretation allows adolescents and adults to develop longer-term purposes for themselves and make plans to achieve them. As goal-oriented, imaginative, and reflective agents, they are able to develop their own identities and styles, even as they continue to harvest the social and psychological riches available through their coordinated interactivity and inter-subjectivity with others. Through these social interactions and experiences, we emerge through childhood and adolescence as persons with distinctive identities, self-awareness, creative possibility, and rational and moral agency. As person agents we are able to exercise some degree of self-determination, even if we do not always think or choose to do so and even as we continue to be shaped and influenced by the words and actions of others and the world around us.

The human agency exercised by persons who are the subjects of psychological research makes them different from the phenomena of natural science. Together with Jeff Sugarman and others (Martin & Sugarman, 1999; Martin, Sugarman, & Thompson, 2003; Martin, Sugarman, & Hickinbottom, 2010), I have spent much of my academic life attempting to understand exactly what the implications of human agency are for psychological inquiry and practice, a task complicated by what I only can describe as a deeply ambivalent and at least somewhat incoherent conception of human agency held by psychologists, one that seems to differ depending to a great extent on whether psychologists view persons as subjects in their research or recipients of their professional services, which they mostly claim are based on their research findings. As researchers, psychologists want to establish law-like regularities governing psychological phenomena. In order to do this, they must assume that the actions and experiences of persons are under the deterministic control of external and internal factors of which persons themselves are not fully aware or able to control. However, as professional service providers, psychologists must assume that persons, aided by the therapeutic ministrations of psychologists, can be made aware of and use their understanding of such factors (and the presumed regularities that govern them) as revealed by psychological research and clinical expertise. In other words, when going about their daily lives or when participating in psychological research, persons are considered by psychologists to have very limited agency, understood as the ability to choose and enact actions based on their choices and purposes. However, once expert psychologists enter the picture as therapists, persons with whom they work are understood to have the capability of self-determination, somehow granted to them by the research-based psychological interventions they participate in. This is an incoherent and self-serving picture of persons as agents. Is psychological expertise based on such powerful and generalizable knowledge that it can enable persons who lack agency to be transformed miraculously into comparatively robust agents capable of exercising a self-determination that can override the uncontrollable internal and external determinants to which they previously had been held hostage? From what has been said thus far, this seems extremely unlikely.

Clearly, if the best that psychological research can supply are generalizations that admit to exceptions such that they cannot speak directly to individuals and always must be tailored to particular situations, how can this research serve as a reliable basis for the therapeutic transformation of non-agents into strong agents? It seems much more reasonable to suggest that persons are agents before and after exposure to psychological research and intervention, but that their agency never is complete and often is not exercised due to any number of possible confusions and restrictions, some of which might be reduced or alleviated by various interactions including but not restricted to those with professional psychologists. The most likely way out of this quagmire is to accept that persons can be more or less self-determining depending on their life experiences and what they make of them and as such they always can react to and interact within interpersonal, social situations in unpredictable ways.

A key point here is one made by Ian Hacking (1995). Persons can be affected by, interact with, and react to how they are treated and classified in ways and to extents that inanimate objects and other animals cannot. If a person becomes aware that she is upsetting her friends by being depressed in their company, she may decide to "put on a good face," stop getting together with them, apologize and ask for their forbearance, or engage in any number of other ways of dealing with or avoiding the situation. Neither psychological research nor professional expertise can predict or determine with lawful regularity which of such outcomes will occur in any particular situation for any particular person. By playing fast and loose with the granting of agency to persons depending on whether or not they are participants in research or clients in therapy, psychologists and organized psychology effectively grant themselves the right to pronounce upon and intervene in the lives of other persons. By disguising the bald facts of this reality to themselves, they allow themselves to join a long line of reductionists and manipulators who effectively, to paraphrase Rüdiger Safranski (1998), think of persons as small so that they can do great things with them. Human interaction is not material interaction. Two people interacting is not like two balls colliding or two chemicals combining. The autonomy, individuality, and agency of persons do not admit readily to the kind of lawful regularities achieved in some branches of natural science.

And yet, taking seriously the agency of persons should not entail any valorization of the inner, private lives of persons over their social lives with others. It is our life experience with others in our families, communities, societies, and cultures that allows us to develop as persons throughout our individual life histories. To ignore the power of social, political, economic, and moral practices and traditions that shape and enable our developmental emergence as agentive persons would be both theoretically and empirically impossible and court a kind of solipsism. When psychologists purport to be able to access and measure so-called internal entities such as personality traits, self structures, and cognitive schemata, there is a great danger that such hypothetical entities, the ontological status of which is unknown, will become reified as the real, root causes of human experience and action. A major step down this road is to assume that such mysterious entities can be calibrated without careful study of the sociocultural contexts within which persons interact and lead their daily lives. When this happens, the social psychological realities of persons become crammed and cramped inside us— some sort of mysterious, inner reality, removed from anyone, save the statistically-aided expert in psychological measurement whose expertise is vetted and sanctioned by professional bodies such as the American Psychological Association and Canadian Psychological Association. The danger here is that if we believe that what makes us who we are is mostly and most basically inside us, it follows that the way forward is to turn inward to determine the validity of our attitudes and actions, not to engage actively and constructively with a world of others. It is only through such engagement that we emerge developmentally as persons and agents. To think otherwise can infect us and our communities with psychologically based individual and group solipsism—an insistence on the social, political, and moral primacy of our uniquely subjective perspectives and emotions, even when such narrow, highly personalized stances trump and disrupt the pluralism and multiperspectivity that the peaceful coexistence and flourishing of persons in common arguably might require.

A personal reflection

Much has been said in this volume about the inability of psychological research that uses aggregated data and statistical methods and procedures to speak directly to the individual person, including some of what I already have said in this chapter. Here I will add only a personal reflection or two concerning this matter. Over many years of conducting and supervising empirical research in education and psychology, I can testify that the statistical methodological assumption of empirical regularities in aggregate data that on closer examination of results for individuals turn out to be non-existent is more the norm than exception in work of this kind. Upon close questioning, most psychologists will admit that individual results of exposure to psychological interventions, strategies, and treatment regimens may differ greatly from results for groups to which these individuals have been assigned or belong. However, they most often vastly underestimate or gloss over the typical magnitude of such variability.

One of my students, Wanda Power (2014), was able to obtain, after much difficulty and many approaches to authors of published research in psychology, raw data from two highly cited empirical studies. When she examined individual data from these studies, like Lamiell (2003), she found almost as many deviations of individual results from the directional results reported for aggregated group data to which the individual results contributed as she did regularities in direction of outcome. For her work, Wanda was awarded the Mary Wright Award for Best Student Paper at the annual conference of the Canadian Psychological Association, Section on History and Philosophy of Psychology. (See James Grice's chapter in this volume for methods of data analysis and report that reveal clearly the extent to which aggregated results apply to the various individuals contributing to them.)

A moment's reflection will suffice to inform us why such discrepancies between empirical research results for individuals and the groups to which they belong are legion. Those who participate in empirical research in psychology are persons with agentive capability. Their interpretations of research instructions and situations inevitably reflect their life experiences. In a study I conducted many years ago (Martin, 1979), I and my research assistant were puzzled by the very different responses high school students had to an experimental intervention we were studying that assumed asking students higher-order questions would help them to think and learn more deeply. When we eventually got around to talking to individual students, we discovered that some students did not respond well to higher-order questions intended to increase their interest and enthusiasm because they assumed the teacher was attempting to show them up, catch them out, or otherwise reprimand them for some reason. Others were confused and did not understand how they were supposed to respond. Still others didn't notice that anything different was going on.

Of course an understanding of what is happening here, and tends to happen in a great deal of educational research, follows from exactly the points made by philosophers like Robin Barrow (1984; Barrow & Foreman, 2005):

> We cannot isolate and control for the various different dimensions to the activity of the individual teacher [and pupil] and we also must recognize that each different student-teacher interaction and combination creates a new possibility. ... I am not suggesting that all researchers are oblivious to these or other problems. But I do think that, generally speaking, the magnitude of the problem has been vastly underestimated.
>
> (Barrow & Foreman, 2005, p. 25)

Exactly so. However, I think it might not be inappropriate to add "and/or purposefully ignored." My own interaction with empirical researchers in psychology tells me that these problems are indeed well known but quietly passed over in the interests of getting on with careers and opportunities, and in doing so, convincing ourselves that problems with the methods employed somehow will not stand in the way of "progress." This being so, the positive proposal with which I wish to end this chapter probably will do nothing to convince most mainstream psychologists to abandon the fallacious idea that statistically analyzed group data are a royal road to a scientific understanding of individual persons.

I have become quite accustomed to being described and dismissed as "anti-science" when I speak to or write about the matters that occupy me herein. For the record, I am not against science. It is pseudo-empiricism and scientism I find misleading and worrisome. In the absence of a bona fide scientific and empirical psychology that speaks to the individual person, I firmly believe that a turn to detailed biographical, life studies of persons will tell us more about individual human beings than any scientistic posturing. Such a turn may not, strictly speaking, be scientific, but it certainly is empirical and directly relevant to individual persons and their lives.

Biography and life writing

If psychologists are truly interested in understanding individual persons in depth, it is odd that so few of them seem interested in one of humankind's most time-honored means of doing so. Biography has been an important form for recording the stories of individual lives since the dawn of recorded literature. It is an old and ubiquitous practice that has taken many forms—biography and autobiography, letters, memoirs, diaries, testimonials, travelogues, journals, confessions, personal essays, case studies, and stories of individual lives told in novels, poetry, conversations and dialogues, scripts, and recorded gossip. These are just some of the forms in which the rich data of individual personhood have found their way into written expression. Non-written forms of life stories such as photography, film, audio recordings, and personal artifacts also can be converted to life writing and expand the range of sources on which such writing can be based and considered. Historiography, guidelines for interviewing, and a host of past and current practices for gathering qualitative data constitute and contribute methodologically to the ancient and ever-changing narrative character and potential of life writing. To capture the protean character of writing about lives, the *Encyclopedia of Life Writing: Autobiographical and Biographical Forms* (Jolly, 2017) includes well over 600 entries. That psychology, which claims knowledge of the experience and actions of individual human beings as its disciplinary reach and purpose, should almost completely ignore this rich source of data is astounding. That it should replace such richness so entirely with an empirical research literature *mostly* silent about the individual lives of persons reveals much more about the scientific ambitions of its practitioners than conveying any convincing concern for comprehending the life stories and contexts within which persons exist and develop as socially spawned psychological beings.

Having said this, it would be wrong to suggest that life writing has been *entirely* ignored by psychologists. Examples of psychological uses of life writing include the use of biography and autobiography in the history of psychology and in the psychology of creativity, the use of case studies in clinical psychology and psychotherapy, documentation of individual life trajectories in developmental and personality psychology, and an increasing interest in narrative psychology. Currently there are signs that psychology, or at least a growing number of psychologists, is finally recognizing the potential of life writing for advancing its understanding of persons and the human condition. A ninth volume in the series *A History of Psychology in Autobiography* has been published. The flagship journal of the American Psychological Association, *American Psychologist*, recently published a special issue on psycho-biography. A new society, *The Society for Qualitative Research in Psychology*, has been established and book series in narrative psychology have begun to appear (e.g., The Oxford Series "Explorations in Narrative Psychology" edited by Mark Freeman). Of course, not all qualitative or narrative research in psychology or elsewhere focuses on individual persons within their particular life contexts, but there are increasing examples of work that does exactly this. If any psychologist interested in life writing is willing to go beyond the borders of disciplinary psychology, she or he easily can access the extensive literature of life writing described so briefly here.

In my own foray into life writing, I have turned to a social psychological form of psycho-biography. Traditionally, psychodynamic psycho-biography has used Freudian or Eriksonian lenses to interpret interpersonal activity and intrapersonal experience in the lives of individuals. In an attempt to ensure adequate recognition of the broader social and cultural contexts within which the subjects of my psycho-biographical studies existed, lived, and worked, I have used the social psychology of George Herbert Mead, especially his conceptions of particular and generalized others. I've then added further emphases on the human existential condition and the materiality of social contexts— that is, while sharing, with more traditional work in psycho-biography, a strong focus on interpersonal interactions, I also consider transactions of a focal person within the human condition writ large and within social institutions, traditions, technologies, and materials, from texts to machines.

In the past ten years, I have conducted dual psycho-biographies of important but contrasting figures in the history of psychology. Using a Meadian social developmental theory of social position exchange (cf. Martin & Gillespie, 2010) and the method of life positioning analysis (Martin, 2013, 2015), I have conducted dual biographical studies of Stanley Milgram's and Ernest Becker's lives as related to their very different theories of evil, and of Carl Rogers' and B. F. Skinner's lives as related to their theories of human freedom and control. In both studies, I have linked prototypic and often repeated interpersonal interactions and social exchanges experienced by each of these individuals to the theoretical frameworks and methodological practices they employed in their psychological inquiries.

Very briefly, both Becker and Milgram, partially as a result of their personal and familial experiences leading up to, during, and following the Second World War, were concerned about the human potential for and actuality of evil. Both used their own, very different career paths and methods to uncover what they regarded as some of the root causes of evil—*obedience to authority* for Milgram and *immortality striving*, combined with his concept of *cultures as immortality projects*, for Becker. Notably, Becker's primary career objective was to construct what he called an "*ideal/real theory of democracy* in which each person strives to achieve *maximum individuality within maximum community*" (Liechty, 2005, p. 19). In different ways, it can be argued that Becker and

Milgram were Enlightenment scholars who believed in the potential of their work for enhancing human understanding and betterment, despite the apparently enduring recesses of evil they attempted to illuminate.

The perspectives that both Rogers and Skinner developed to deal with social challenges they experienced in their own lives, with family and others, were in many ways indistinguishable from those they applied in their psychological inquiries and theories and in their later life attempts to *save the world*. In both life and work, Rogers experienced difficulty moving easily between the social positions of speaker and listener, finding it especially difficult to express himself openly to others, particularly, and oddly given his work, around issues of intimacy. Skinner, on the other hand, struggled with tensions related to social positions of controlling positively and being controlled punitively, experiencing strongly and personally the adaptive functions of the former in contrast to the maladaptive personal and social consequences of the latter. Both Skinner's utopian social engineering and Roger's efforts to encourage personal, interpersonal, and world peace are quite reasonably interpretable as attempts to enable appropriate and viable levels of individual freedom and control, together with positive social development, despite their very different contours.

I believe that psycho-biography is especially applicable to the illumination of two pivotal matters in the psychology of personhood: (1) the developmental emergence of social psychological aspects of persons (e.g., self and other understanding, social and personal identity, perspective taking, moral and rational agency, and character and comportment) and (2) the study of individual lives in ways that might warrant provisional, yet productive speculation concerning persons more generally. Each psycho-biographical study constitutes a possibility for human being that potentially enriches our sense of available options for living satisfying and productive lives. In my own work, I attempt to pay particular attention to relations between interactivity and inter-subjectivity, as well as to the social and material contexts within which persons exist and act.

A final personal note

At this late stage in my career, I find myself turning more and more to the humanities for depictions of the person in full. The best humanities scholarship probes carefully and peers deeply into human lives in ways that capture their uniqueness, and yet communicate something beyond singularity. An Elizabeth Strout novel or a short story by Alice Munro puts the reader immediately and powerfully into lives that are unrepeatable, but somehow familiar. It is possible to learn much from such particulars, even while knowing the experiences being imbibed are not one's own; yet somehow in the midst of these singularities you also feel connected, not just to the characters you are reading about, but to certain aspects of human "being" writ large—knowing the final fate of all protagonists is one you share (in outcome, if not in manner) and feeling the frustrations and triumphs of strivings that are inevitable and cannot be avoided in any life with others.

By immersing myself in a wider variety of life writings, I have learned much that escaped me in the first twenty years of my professional life as an applied and academic psychologist, plying the methodological tools and perspectives of a conventional psychological researcher and practitioner. Through my biographical and psycho-biographical studies, I have learned and understood things about being a person that have affected me in beneficial ways. Having immersed myself in the details of a few lives, I feel more connected to aspects of my self that I previously glimpsed but did not probe. I also feel more attuned to people in general.

As William Stern (1911) realized over 100 years ago, "it is only through an artistic, empathic synthesis that a genuine [understanding of life] emerges" (p. 329). It was precisely such a realization that Sigmund Koch urged on psychologists many years later, pleading for them to "finally accept the circumstance that extensive and important sectors of psychological study require modes of inquiry rather more like those of the humanities than the sciences" (p. 416). Biography and psycho-biography do not exhaust the psychological relevance of the humanities or the plethora of approaches to life writing that are available but they can contribute to an understanding of persons and our lives—what I believe psychology ought to do, but seldom does as currently practiced.

References

Barrow, R. (1984). *Giving teaching back to teachers: A critical introduction to curriculum theory.* Brighton: Wheatsheaf Books and London, ON: Althouse Press.

Barrow, R., & Foreman-Peck, L. (2005). *What use is educational research? A debate.* London: Philosophy of Education Society of Great Britain.

Hacking, I. (1995). *Rewriting the soul: Multiple personality and the sciences of memory.* Princeton, NJ: Princeton University Press.

Jolly, M. (Ed.). (2017). *Encyclopedia of life writing: Autobiographical and biographical forms.* London: Routledge.

Koch, S. (1999). *Psychology in human context: Essays in dissidence and reconstruction.* D. Finkelman & F. Kessel (Eds.). Chicago: University of Chicago Press.

Lamiell, J. T. (2003). *Beyond individual and group differences: Human individuality, scientific psychology, and William Stern's* Critical Personalism. Thousand Oaks, CA: Sage.

Liechty, D. (2005). Introduction. In D. Liechty (Ed.), *The Ernest Becker reader.* (pp. 1–23). Seattle: The University of Washington Press.

Martin, J. (1979). Effects of teacher higher-order questions on student process and product variables in a single classroom study. *Journal of Educational Research, 72,* 183–187.

Martin, J. (2013). Life positioning analysis: An analytic framework for the study of lives and life narratives. *Journal of Theoretical and Philosophical Psychology, 33,* 1–17.

Martin, J. (2015). Life positioning analysis. In J. Martin, J. Sugarman, & K. L. Slaney (Eds.), *The Wiley handbook of theoretical and philosophical psychology: Methods, approaches, and new directions for social sciences* (pp. 248–262). Oxford: Wiley Blackwell.

Martin, J. (2016). Ernest Becker and Stanley Milgram: Twentieth century students of evil. *History of Psychology, 19,* 3–21.

Martin, J. (2017). Carl Rogers' and B. F. Skinner's approaches to personal and societal improvement: A study in the psychological humanities. *Journal of Theoretical and Philosophical Psychology, 37,* 214–229.

Martin, J., & Gillespie, A. (2010). A neo-Meadian approach to human agency: Relating the social and the psychological in the ontogenesis of perspective coordinating persons. *Integrative Psychological and Behavioral Science, 44,* 252–272.

Martin, J., & Sugarman, J. (1999). *The psychology of human possibility and constraint.* Albany: State University of New York Press.

Martin, J., & Sugarman, J. (2009). Does interpretation in psychology differ from interpretation in natural science? *The Journal for the Theory of Social Behaviour, 39,* 19–37.

Martin, J., Sugarman, J., & Hickinbottom, S. (2010). *Persons: Understanding psychological selfhood and agency.* New York: Springer.

Martin, J., Sugarman, J., & Thompson, J. (2003). *Psychology and the question of agency.* Albany: State University of New York Press.

Mead, G. H. (1934). *Mind, self, and society from the standpoint of a social behaviorist.* Chicago: University of Chicago Press.

Power, W. (June 2014). Self-determination theory: A critical analysis. In K. L. Slaney & T. P. Racine (Chairs), *History and philosophy of psychology across the spectrum.* Symposium presented at the annual meeting of the Canadian Psychological Association, Vancouver, BC, Canada.

Safranski, R. (1998). Martin Heidegger: Between good and evil *(E. Osers, Trans.).* Cambridge, MA: Harvard University Press.

Stern, W. (1911). *Die differentielle psychologie in ihren methodischen Grundlagen* [*Methodological foundations of differential psychology*]. Leipzig: Barth.

Tomasello, M. (1999). *The cultural origins of human cognition.* Cambridge, MA: Harvard University Press.

Vasello, S. (2013). *Self-regulated learning: An application of critical educational psychology.* New York: Peter Lang.

9 Summary and commentary on *Scientific Psychology's Troubling Inertia*

Lisa M. Osbeck

Evident from the plot of Shakespeare's *Measure for Measure* is an historical meaning of "measure" to connote evaluation or judgment, as in a weighing of the worth of human acts. I make the reference here because the authors contributing to this volume collectively level a damning 'measure' (evaluation) of their field and what are broadly construed as its measurement practices. In response to the authors' general assessment that psychology continues to employ unsound and unsuitable methods in the face of decades of incisive critique, I am reminded of a well-known line from that play: "Some rise by sin and some by virtue fall" (Act 2 Scene 1).

For this final chapter, the editors have requested that I offer brief commentary on the effectiveness of the arguments and the overall project of the volume. I am happy to do so, but only after first expressing my abiding respect for the authors and my sympathy for the cause undertaken. I will share what I take to be most significant contributions from the chapters and what is similar and different across them, followed by observations and comments from my reading of the text as a whole.

Summary of chapter contributions

James Lamiell details what he labels an "interpretive (mal)practice": the use of aggregate statistics to forward knowledge claims about individual persons. With detailed historical analysis and pertinent text examples Lamiell documents a critical reaction to this misuse of aggregate data dating to at least the mid-20th century. However, the reproof has done little to deter the practice. Lamiell also reveals historical developments that contributed to the problem in the first place, rooted in a confusing shift in disciplinary focus from *individuals* to individual differences. The latter, entailing population level analysis, was originally conceived and described by Stern as a *complement* to rather than substitute for a focus on the unique individual. Instead, focus on individual differences has superseded efforts to understand the unique individual. Thus, we might say that personality is the research area for which population statistics have been perhaps most egregiously misappropriated. Drawing on difficult episodes from his own experience, Lamiell describes his personal quest to influence the field of personality research for the better. Lamiell's denunciation of "statisticism" implicates psychology's sanctioned research practices as they are passed down and retained. Yet these practices stem from and reflect conceptual error. Personality as a subfield exhibits a fundamental misunderstanding of the difference between the two levels of analysis, with consequences that have regrettably impacted the field (psychology) at large. Special problems ensue when the misconceptions engender misapplications, as when psychological appraisal, assessment, or therapeutic recommendations are made for individuals on the basis of findings derived only from the aggregate – from populations. It is easy to understand Lamiell's apparent frustration. He has been a hard-hitting critic over four decades, successfully sounding the alarm in outlets as prominent as *American Psychologist*, and from a position as highly respected scholar and personality researcher. His concerns have not been heeded by the field at large and instead have launched several instances of counter critique, the (in)adequacy of which Lamiell critiques in turn. His own experience as well has historical insights give Lamiell reason to consider psychological science to be incorrigible – unresponsive to critique, unrepentant, and unreflective.

Lamiell's contention that psychology's methodological problems are not merely due to execution but to fundamental (mis) conception fittingly sets up Fiona Hibberd's chapter, a scathing condemnation of psychological science's long-standing neglect or rejection of conceptual analysis, the logical analysis of relations. Hibberd views this failure as "not wanting to know," calling it a "forceful and sustained resistance" (p. 10). She is nuanced on the question of whether the neglect is intentional, but it is unquestionably an ethical matter in her view. In addition, Hibberd's critique strongly suggests that psychology's empirical foundation is deficient. She argues that the discipline's conceptual vacuum, its failure to engage in conceptual testing and analysis makes for second-rate science. This is ironic given that the pretense of methodological rigor historically justifies psychology's claims to scientific standing. Hibberd reminds us that conceptual analysis is indispensable to science; it aids empirical investigation by establishing a sound foundation – providing "the best conceptual material" for empirical analysis

(p. 6), including such basic concepts as that of "evidence" itself. Hibberd reminds us that science progresses only by means of a continual process of self-correction. By implication, then, psychological science is on course for failure as an intellectual and empirical enterprise. Although she sees no change or ready solution forthcoming, she imagines the possibility of impact through collaboration, specifically an authoritative paper affirming the fundamental role of conceptual analysis in any science including psychology. Hibberd acknowledges that authors contributing to such a manifesto would need to downplay their differences in the interests of establishing a unified front; moreover, she doubts that the intended audience would receive the paper well. She stresses that education is also indispensable, not on an incidental basis but in the form of a coordinated educational *campaign*.

Richard Hohn focuses on the (in)coherence of one specific concept central to psychological science, that of measurement. He mines the seminal historical analysis of measurement concepts by Joel Michell to argue that psychology has been "incorrigible" with respect to its treatment of measurement, resulting in a series of traceable "missteps" (Hohn, this volume, p.39), the first of which was to assume without testing the assumption that psychological phenomena are inherently subject to quantification and measurement. Hohn targets S. S. Stevens's well-known and highly influential redefinition of measurement as especially consequential in that it enabled a conception of measurement so broad or opaque that any empirical analysis could qualify. But the burden of blame is shared by the wider community of psychologists content to let a radical redefinition of measurement pass without substantive comment. Hohn notes, however, that measurement theory continued to progress during the years Stevens' measurement concept was incorporated into existing frameworks and practices. Innovations in measurement theory and alternative models emerged, yet the impact of these efforts on psychological science remains minimal. Drawing a link between psychology's inattention to this midcentury theoretical progress and a widespread neglect of Michell's recent critique, Hohn notes a similar lack of impact outside of specialized circles, and whether unnoticed or dismissed, Michell's critique had little impact on disciplinary practices. Hohn suggests that psychology's overall "momentum" fueled by an appetite for perceived scientific advancement and practical significance function to derail any substantive challenge to its fundamental methods and conceptions. Yet, like Hibberd, Hohn argues that this pattern threatens the very scientific foundation it seeks to protect, given that a genuine science thrives on self-critical scrutiny and improvement. Also in agreement with Hibberd, Hohn urges intervention through education, specifically through cultivation of critical thinking in psychology courses, including methods.

A fitting follow-up to Hohn's analysis of problematic conceptions of psychological measurement, James Grice, Huntjen, and Johnson's chapter highlights the entrenched disciplinary use of Null Hypothesis Significance Testing (NHST), to make population level inferences from samples. That this practice is shared with other fields that use population statistics does little to alleviate its problematical standing. In the case of psychology, the practice continues despite years of targeted and even officially sanctioned criticism. Grice and coauthors thus doubt whether recent official admonitions of NHST and the routine reporting of p-values (Wasserstein & Lazar, 2016; Wasserstein, Schirm & Lazar, 2019) will have any genuine impact on practice trends in psychology at large. In the face of what they regard as a widespread conflation of statistical with scientific reasoning on the part of psychologists, Grice et al. endorse a shift in emphasis away from statistical inference to a broader focus on scientific explanation. Such a change would entail attention to the fact that *persons* engage in reasoning activities that enable the accumulation of knowledge and the advancement of any science. How could such a fundamental alteration within the discipline be achieved? Grice and coauthors suggest that working with what is familiar to and thus comfortable for psychologists may be the best way of introducing models that could serve as alternatives to NHST. Grice's own Observation-Oriented Modeling (OOM) approach (Grice, 2011) serves as an example and an especially promising option. The OOM model is person-centered, informed by both scientists' senses (visualization) and a working causal theory; it relies on abductive rather than merely statistical reasoning. It is in these ways that OOM has deep roots in conceptions of empirical science that date to Aristotle; it is consistent with a historically and philosophically informed, broad but rigorous conception of scientific practice.

The expansive person-centered model of scientific reasoning emerging with OOM is the appropriate framework within which to best appreciate the contributions of Donna Tafreshi's chapter. Tafreshi elucidates the interpretive acts inherent in and essential to quantitative analysis, despite the widespread practice of distinguishing qualitative methods from quantitative on the grounds that the former are "interpretive" methods. Both quantitative and qualitative researchers tend to make this assumption, propagating an unhelpful, even harmful division between qualitative and quantitative. Like Hohn and Hibberd, Tafreshi sees promise for correction through education, encouraging students to appreciate that methods are tools persons use and misuse for a variety of purposes. Demonstrated in her analysis of well-selected historical examples is that interpretive activities occur in the context of communities, and always with historically contingent contexts conventions and agendas.

Yet students' readiness to receive such encouragement may be questioned if Kathleen Slaney is right that the psychological community demonstrates little "appetite" for critique. Slaney regards critical methodology as a subdiscipline in psychology, one with its own long history and a strong relation to proclamations of a disciplinary "crisis." She proposes three categories of critique within this historical context: (1) condemning misunderstanding and misapplications of methods within a fairly circumscribed conceptual and practice space, for example a particular method misused in a particular context; (2) calling for more sweeping methodological changes needed to establish psychology on a more rigorous scientific foundation; and (3) dismantling natural science and its ontological and epistemological assumptions as a basis for psychological theorizing. Through analysis of historical exemplars (critics) in each category Slaney acknowledges that the boundaries of her categories are blurry. In turn she proposes that the three categories might be subsumed under the superordinate headings of restitutive and radical approaches to critique. The first two categories reflect criticism that retains a commitment to psychology as science, with the goal of making psychology a better science with greater methodological integrity (thus "restitutive"). The third category entails criticism that rejects the entire theoretical foundation and calls for an overthrow, a reconceptualization of psychology as something other than a branch of the sciences (thus "radical"). Slaney notes that where psychology has responded to critique, this has come in the form of small corrective steps taken in the interests of restitution. Reflecting on the reasons broader criticisms have failed to take hold, Slaney describes what she calls a "disconnection" between psychologists who conduct research in the trenches and those who theorize about it (methodologists), with most practicing psychologists unaware of and unaffected by critical stances. She suggests several system level reasons for the disconnect: incomplete or insufficient methodological training, lack of access to adequate software, and little exposure to methods of critical analysis, resulting in an inability to engage with critical literature; a publish or perish educational culture and lack of interest and support for critical work on the part of editors and review boards. As I read her analysis, prognosis is grim, with small and relatively inconsequential adjustments much more likely than conceptual and methodological overhaul.

Nevertheless, Jack Martin's paper directs our focus back around to the unique individual, the person, and the grounds of possibility of knowledge of persons, which requires more extensive disciplinary upheaval. For Martin, knowledge of persons is not likely to be generated by traditional psychological methods that proceed from a search for universal regularities, given the exploration of particularities of disposition, interaction, and context required by a person-centered agenda. Instead, inspiration for methods adequate for understanding persons springs from the humanities, especially fine-grained and highly contextualized bibliographical study: life histories. This conclusion Martin has drawn from a career spent in careful consideration of precisely what human agency implies and requires for psychological research and practice. He emphasizes that foregrounding agency obliges both exploration of private experience and analysis of cultural and institutional contexts that give rise, support, maintain, and modify it. As illustrated through his own recent study of B. F. Skinner and Carl Rogers, Martin offers a seemingly novel consolidation of psychobiographical method with the social theory of George Herbert Mead. This connection to Mead's theory enables Martin to suggest that the study of lives provides grounding not only for revealing the social dimensions of particular lives, but also offers a basis upon which to collate a repertoire of possibilities for human experience and action, enabling psychological understanding on a more general scale.

Similarities and differences across chapters

Clearly each chapter in this volume offers important insights and is instructive in its level of detail, making each one a worthy stand-alone contribution. But we may also hope to glean a more collective vision from such a rich assembly. Thus, after summarizing the unique themes from each chapter, what generalizations might we make about the volume as a whole? First, of course, there is general agreement across the chapters that psychology has shown a consistent historical pattern of relying on problematic or inappropriate methods and that it is unamenable to reform in the face of critique. Nevertheless, we find some dissimilarities across chapters. These are best understood as differences of emphasis rather than spirit or substance. To highlight these small divergences, we may distinguish a set of sub-questions the authors implicitly address:

First, *what is the core problem with psychology*? That is, what specific disciplinary practices does the author target as especially troubling; what methods, traditions, assumptions, or omissions are most lamentable? We find an emphasis on the problem of drawing inferences to persons from population level statistics (Lamiell), on conflating statistical with scientific reasoning (Grice), a distain for conceptual analysis in general (Hibberd), a pervasive misconception of "measurement," specifically (Hohn), a failure to appreciate the interpretive aspects of quantitative analysis (Tafreshi), a general distaste for critique (Slaney), and an inadequate basis for analysis of context and interaction over time and situation conducive to understanding persons (Martin). One could argue that all of these problems overlap and are interactive, but they are at least in principle distinguishable features of the discipline and we should avoid a temptation to collapse them into one disciplinary mess.

Second, *what are the reasons for the problems identified?* How does each author account for what gave rise to or sustains the problem(s) targeted in the chapter? Authors point to different historical/scholarly/disciplinary developments and seem to wrestle with the question of whether disciplinary patterns most accurately reflect a lack of access to critique on the part of most psychologists, an inability to process or engage with available critique (i.e., because education in psychology does not promote the requisite critical thinking skills), lack of interest in meta-theory, chronic resistance to change, or a value system that prioritizes tangible practical outcome at the expense of epistemic integrity.

Third, *what can be done about psychology's problems and errors?* What reformative measures can be taken, if any to advance more adequate methods and practices? Different answers to this question reflect to some extent the different reasons given for the problem in the first place. Lack of access to critique would indicate a very different course of action than would chronic resistance. Ignorance would require raising awareness; confusion calls for efforts at clarification. Changing a broad value system is most difficult of all and may require detailed analysis of what sustains the values in the current system. In the face of the various possibilities for understanding the source of psychology's problems, chapter authors offer tentative suggestions for reform. Hibberd suggests that publishing a multi-authored manifesto might be effective, but only if the publication has a high level of visibility and impact. She also stresses the importance of educating students in existing debates and honing their critical thinking skills, which Hohn and Tafreshi similarly emphasize. Grice advocates *demonstration* of the usefulness of alternative models and methods; he also notes the importance of communicating in language psychologists will easily understand. We might put all of these suggestions together to develop a multi-tiered intervention, but the specifics of such an approach require much additional thought.

Finally, what is the *overarching goal* of the author's critique? Here it would seem beneficial to apply to the chapters the same categories

Kathleen Slaney used to distinguish forms or levels of critique as they have been aimed at psychology historically. For example, to appreciate ways quantitative analysis involves interpretation is perhaps a restitutive goal, but reinterpreting psychology as a branch of the humanities encompasses a more radical agenda. Nevertheless, I find it difficult to divide the authors' arguments cleanly into restitutive and radical agendas. There are restitutive aspects and radical aspects alike in every case, or perhaps we might say that although offered in the spirit of restitution the reforms proposed are of such a nature that radical upheaval is the logical end. This suggests that the authors have individually and collectively accomplished their goal of persuading at least this reader that psychology's disciplinary and scientific integrity is compromised in both basic and applied research both because of its methods and the persistent conceptual snags that accompany their pervasive use. That psychology's failure to respond meaningfully to critical evaluation provides little basis for anticipating future redirection and reform is a further conclusion we can draw from consideration of the chapters as a set. In offering its arguments, the book accomplishes an additional task: it conveys both focused and broad views of some of psychology's historical and contemporary problems of method, providing a useful educational resource for students freshly and challenging seasoned scholars with fresh perspectives on the discipline in which they have been "trained."

Observations and comments

Despite my appreciation of the chapters individually and the volume as a whole, I will share a few questions, observations, and suggestions. First, as noted, authors seem to grapple with the best way to characterize psychology's problematic tendencies. Is it ignorance, confusion, obstinacy, inertia, comfort, incorrigibility, recalcitrance, disregard? I was struck by the fact that many of the adjectives that authors use to characterize psychology as a discipline or set of practices are qualities typically used to describe persons; that is, they are dispositional attributes. What is the problem with invoking personal attributes to characterize psychology as a discipline? For one thing, it could be taken as reflective of a category mistake, given that dispositional attitudes properly belong to another ontological kind (Ryle, 1949). Persons can be described as ignorant or stubborn or confused, but disciplines cannot, at least not in a literal sense. If this point seems pedantic, it is worth remembering that a claim made forcefully and compellingly in this volume is that it is

124   *Lisa M. Osbeck*

problematic to use population level statistics to make knowledge claims about individuals. An implication is that persons and populations are different in kind and that attributions applicable to one are not suitable to the other. Thus, the use of personal attributes to characterize widespread disciplinary practice over time might be charged with demonstrating a similar slippage, unintentional as it is. Including myself in the project of this volume, we must take care to avoid the appearance of moving from one ontological category to another without explicit recognition that one is doing so metaphorically or with some other justification in mind. If it is merely a "manner of speaking," we do so at some risk of being misunderstood.

A closely related problem with invoking personal attributes to describe psychology's historical woes is the suggestion, however inadvertent, that the fault lies with persons rather than the systems within which persons act. We may recognize that successful adaptation to a problematic system perpetuates problems in that system yet remain sympathetic to the needs and experiences of goal-directed persons acting within it. Consider the case of a typical ambitious and compassionate student who desires to "help people" by pursuing a career oriented around clinical assessment and psychotherapy. She studies mightily for the GRE exams, applies herself diligently to her coursework and solicits feedback and guidance from clinical supervisors. She masters the statistical methods and principles of research design presented to her and is encouraged to equate their use with best practices in her field; she continues to rely on research using these statistics to inform her therapy practice. At no point is she encouraged to challenge underlying assumptions and to do so would threaten her career goals. Of course, it is for this very reason that several of the authors underscore the importance of education in the face of problematic disciplinary trends. Similarly, consider the case of a newly minted graduate of a PhD program in psychology fortunate enough to secure a position as assistant professor. She may be required to submit grant applications, pass peer review to publish original research, teach content approved by her colleagues, and pursue name recognition through participation in official disciplinary organizations. It is in principle possible for her to pursue these objectives in the interests of obtaining tenure while privately rejecting the normative and epistemic framework supporting them, but we might wonder how such a discordance could impact the quality of her work or further, even damage her well-being. At what point is she to be blamed for enduring in a tradition that has supported her advancement toward her goals to date? In both cases we might recognize that in a very real sense one's personal goals (a successful career) are tied to perpetuation of sanctioned disciplinary practices, and that these personal goals are embedded in a network of related goals, such as providing for one's children, supporting clients or mentoring students. I do not mean to assert that any of the authors explicitly blames individual persons for the problems described, only that the ways of talking about the problem can suggest inadvertently blame and moral failing directed at the level of persons.

I fully believe that all of the authors contributing to this fine volume blame systems of practice (education and training of psychologists, publication criteria, inherited norms and values) for psychology's troubles. In some cases, such a system level analysis is explicit; for example several chapter authors point to psychologists' prevailing interest in practical outcomes and psychology's thirst for scientific significance. Also, the title's reference to "inertia" suggests a system level attribution. Certainly, we cannot draw a definitive line between persons and the systems that situate them. The self-correction of the system is advanced by scientists and scholars subjecting them*selves* and their practices to continual scrutiny. Be that as it may, problems arising from and sustained within systems call for descriptions of *interaction* and patterns of communication that engender problematic habits, norms, and values. We may surely focus on one or another aspect of the system for sake of clarification and analysis, but the system itself should remain in the foreground. To be explicit, I am suggesting that we require a fuller understanding of why psychological scientists continue to practice in ways that have been deemed problematic, and this understanding requires fine-grained insight into the systems that sustain those practices. In addition to requiring different adjectives – descriptors at the level of interaction and communication, systems level analysis may benefit from consultation with sociology of science and science and technology studies (STS), borrowing frameworks derived for the purpose of analysis of science as a system. It is worth remembering that systems evolve continuously, and thus reasons that were initially factors in the adoption of problematic practices are not necessarily the most important factors at present. As an example of an influence that is specific to the contemporary context, psychologists have been asked to "advocate" for psychology in the APA strategic plan (www.apa.org/about/apa/strategic-plan/index) and are encouraged to "celebrate" psychology and its accomplishments as well as its potential to address new challenges (www.apa.org/topics/covid-19/celebrate-psychology). Resistance to embracing critique can be understood more easily against such messaging and the sentiment it expresses.

Not only sociology of science and cultural studies but the broader History and Philosophy of Science (HPS) tradition can be a useful ally in developing strategies for understanding factors that sustain psychological science as a cultural system. For years analysis of science has been aided by informed historical analysis, especially focusing on concrete episodes of practice (e.g., Kuhn, 1962). The authors in this volume, like historians of psychology more generally, make excellent use of these empirical tools (with historical episodes understood as "data"). However, recent trends in philosophy of science also embrace empirical methods including qualitative analysis and ethnography (e.g., see Wagenknecht, Nersessian, & Andersen, 2015). Theoretical and critical psychology may also benefit from methods for interpreting situated practices in real world contexts, that is, "in the wild" (Hutchins, 1995). It may be informative to collect accounts from psychological scientists concerning the assumptions and values that sustain their commitments to specific methods, and from observational studies of functioning psychological laboratories, clinics, and classrooms. Studies of this kind help to reveal the specific ways cultural meanings (the culture of the discipline) and traditions enable, even require practices critics deem problematic, helping to reveal deep cultural sources of what seem to be incorrigible, intractable patterns. These methods may also offer helpful case studies, accounts from psychologists in different specialties and circumstances to offer a catalog of reasons psychological scientists might cling to outmoded practices against the availability of sound critique. On that note, it seems important for theoretical and critical psychologists to participate more fully in the broader network of HPS than has historically been the case.

However, HPS projects generally do not aim at reforming the science analyzed (de Freitas Araujo, 2017) and this is a crucial difference from critical/theoretical psychology. Given the goal of reform shared by the authors of this volume, several additional points are worth making. First, critique is more effective when accompanied by a constructive alternative, specific models and methods that offer a more robust and ultimately "useful" approach to psychological science. Of course, new models come with no guarantee that colleagues will adopt them, as Lamiell might testify on the basis of many exasperating experiences. James Grice, however, seems more optimistic, having confirmed the benefit of Observation-Oriented Modeling in a variety of applications (e.g., Grice, 2011, 2015). We may take from his enthusiasm the important point that alternative models and methods are most convincing when their problem-solving value is demonstrated, especially in a community (psychology) that values tangible and practical outcomes. Similarly,

Jack Martin's paper shares examples of the method he advocates as a way of demonstrating their relevance. A related point from Grice and coauthors' chapter is that critics should speak in a language that will be understood. This point Slaney also makes by questioning whether psychologists trained in traditional methods will find critical commentary sufficiently accessible. We might also add that it is important to communicate in a manner that will be perceived as valuable by those one attempts to persuade. It is quite possible that the kind of communication that is capable of being received will result only in small or incremental changes, but these changes can accumulate and proliferate over time.

A final observation for the reader is that the focus of the current volume is epistemological, though ethical concerns for psychology emerge as a consequence of faulty epistemology. It bears mentioning that the ethical concerns with psychological methods addressed in this volume concern only a subset of those that have been raised within critical psychology at large. For example, authors of this volume do not take up such issues as systematic racism in psychological science, historically sexist practices, the exclusion of indigenous perspectives, the perpetuation of economic hierarchies, or related problems. These matters are addressed explicitly elsewhere under the broad province of critical psychology (e.g., Teo, 2015). I mention them here only to note that critique of psychological methods historically has addressed additional problems that are not the focus of this volume. However, the exclusion of these topics should not be taken as indication of a lack of concern on the part of this volume's authors, only a decision to focus on another aspect of psychology's troubling inertia for the sake of a different argument.

Undoubtedly, I have left out important details from the authors' arguments and have given what can only be an incomplete perspective on the volume as a whole. Nevertheless, I will end with an expression of gratitude to the editors and authors for the opportunity to engage with the excellent papers, and with hope that my own students and their students will benefit from both the broad and specific insights.

References

de Freitas Araujo, S. (2017). Toward a philosophical history of psychology: An alternative path for the future. *Theory & Psychology, 27*(1), 87–107. https://doi.org/10.1177/0959354316656062.

Grice, J. W. (2011). *Observation oriented modeling: Analysis of cause in the behavioral sciences*. New York: Academic Press.

Grice, J. W. (2015). From means and variances to patterns and persons. *Frontiers in Psychology*, 6:1007. doi: 10.3389/fpsyg.2015.01007.

Hutchins, E. (1995). *Cognition in the wild*. Cambridge, MA: MIT Press.

Kuhn, T. S. (1962). *The structure of scientific revolutions*. Chicago: University of Chicago Press.

Ryle, G., 1949, *The Concept of Mind*, London: Hutchinson University Library.

Teo, T. (2015). Critical psychology: A geography of intellectual engagement and resistance. *American Psychologist*, *70*(3), 243.

Wasserstein, R., & Lazar, N. (2016), The ASA's statement on p-values: Context, process, and purpose. *The American Statistician*, *70*, 129–133.

Wasserstein, R. L., Schirm, A. L., & Lazar, N. A. (2019). Moving to a world beyond "p < 0.05." *The American Statistician*, *73*:sup1, 1–19, DOI: 10.1080/00031305.2019.1583913.

Wagenknecht, S., Nersessian, N. J., & Andersen, H. (2015). Empirical philosophy of science: Introducing qualitative methods into philosophy of science. In Wagenknecht, S., Nersessian, N. J., & Andersen, H. (Eds.), *Empirical philosophy of science* (pp. 1–10). Cham: Springer.

Index

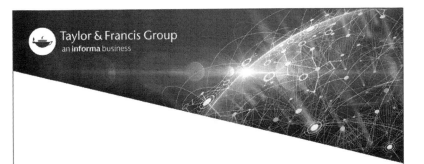

For Product Safety Concerns and Information please contact our EU
representative GPSR@taylorandfrancis.com Taylor & Francis Verlag GmbH,
Kaufingerstraße 24, 80331 München, Germany

Printed and bound by CPI Group (UK) Ltd, Croydon, CR0 4YY

11/04/2025

01844012-0008